New F
Good Pu

CH00621973

Edited by
Mike Power

Power Publications

First published 1995
2nd edition 2001

© **Power Publications**
1 Clayford Ave
Ferndown, Dorset.
BH22 9PQ
www.powerpublications.co.uk

ISBN 1 898073 24 4

Publishers note:
Whilst every care has been taken to ensure that all the
information contained in this book is correct the publishers
cannot accept any responsibility for any inaccuracies that
occur.

Other Local publications
Pub Walks in the New Forest
Mike Power's New Forest Walks
Pub Walks in Hampshire & the IOW
A Mountain Bike Guide to Hampshire and the New Forest

Front cover: The Royal Oak, North Gorley

INTRODUCTION

In 1066 William the Conqueror took over the Saxon forests of Sherwood, Dean, Ashdown etc. but not content, in 1079 he seized the coastal land of Ytene and declared it his new forest known at that time as 'Nova Foresta'.

Today the Forest covers an area of 148 square miles and consists of many diverse landscapes. Up until 1482 there were no inclosures but many now exist and were necessary to protect the growth of young trees. Apart from approximately 30,000 acres of woodland; vast areas of open heath, grass lands, bogs or valley mires and gorse occupy a further 93,000 acres. In January 1992, the government recognised the importance of the New Forest by proposing a status to that of a National Park. Much consultation has taken place as to the precise boundaries and a decision is expected soon.

Administration of the Forest is the responsibility of The Verderers Court the second oldest in the land who still sit six times a year in Queens House, Lyndhurst. Verderers were once officers of the Crown but still play an important part today working with the planning authorities to ensure no developments take place that would be detrimental to the Forest. They appoint 4 agisters who oversee the welfare of the Commoners animals and control and administer the 'Rights of Common'. PASTURE – The right to graze cattle and ponies, TURBARY – The right to dig turf, ESTOVERS – The right to gather firewood, OVERY – The right to keep sheep, MAST – The right to turn out pigs to forage acorns and MARL – The right to dig for lime-rich clay for use as a fertiliser.

In an area of such beauty it is of no surprise to find many hostelries catering for the needs of tourists and locals alike. This illustrated book lists the best of them describing their situation, the type of pub, samples from their menu and their bar list, accommodation details, their opening times and policy with regard to allowing children and dogs on the premises.

With so many pubs in the Forest competition is fierce, sadly some do not survive whilst others change hands on a regular basis. Of those I visited I found the standard generally very high, most had warm winter log fires, a good choice of real ales, a wide range of wines and some excellent, imaginative menus.

The editorial in this book is completely independent; no fee what so ever is paid by any of the pubs to be listed. If you find something you like that we have missed or are disappointed by any aspect please feel free to contact us it will be of great help for future editions.   Mike Power

Contents

31	The Cartwheel Inn	Whitsbury	34
32	The Cat & Fiddle Inn	Hinton Admiral	35
33	The Chequers Inn	Pennington	36
34	The Coach & Horses	Cadnam	37
35	The Compasses Inn	Damerham	37
36	The Crown & Stirrup	Lyndhurst	38
37	The Crown Inn	Everton	39
38	The East End Arms	East End	40
39	The Elm Tree Inn	Ringwood	41
40	The Fighting Cocks	Godshill	42
41	The Filly Inn	Setley	43
42	The Fish Inn	Ringwood	44
43	The Fisherman's Haunt	Winkton	45
44	The Fisherman's Rest	Lymington	46
45	The Forest Heath Hotel	Sway	47
46	The Forest Inn	Ashurst	48
47	The Gamekeper	Woodlands	49
48	The George Inn	Fordingbridge	50
49	The Green Dragon	Brook	51
50	The Gun Inn	Keyhaven	52
51	The High Corner Inn	Linwood	53
52	The Hobler	Battramsley	54
53	The Horse & Groom	Woodreen	55
54	The Jolly Sailor	Ashlet Creek	56
55	The King Rufus	Eling	57
56	The Lamb	Nomansland	58
57	The Lamb Inn	Winkton	59
58	The Master Builder's	Bucklers Hard, Beaulieu	60
59	The Mayflower Inn	Lymington	61
60	The New Queen	Avon	62
61	The Oak Inn	Bank	63
62	The Pilgrim Inn	Marchwood	64
63	The Plough Inn	Tiptoe	65
✓ 64	The Queens Head	Burley	66
65	The Red Lion	Boldre	67

THE NEW FOREST

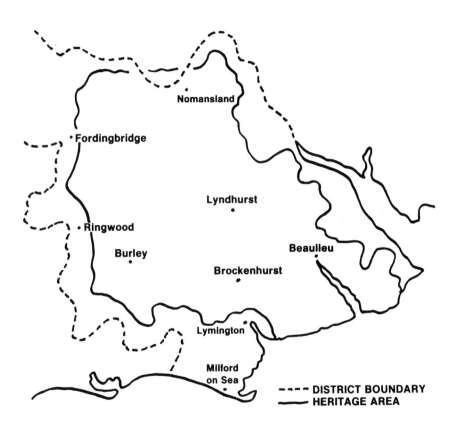

Nomansland

Fordingbridge

Lyndhurst

Ringwood

Burley

Beaulieu

Brockenhurst

Lymington

Milford
on Sea

- - - DISTRICT BOUNDARY
—— HERITAGE AREA

Rockford Green, Ringwood. Tel: 01425 474700. Fax: 483332.

Alice Lisle, the courageous lady after whom this popular Forest inn is named lived in nearby Moyles Court and was sadly beheaded in Winchester for giving refuge to a couple of survivors of Monmouth's rebellion. At her trial the notorious Judge Jeffreys overturned the jury's 'not guilty' verdict and ordered that she be burned at the stake. After a public appeal to James II she was be-headed in Winchester and buried at Ellingham church yard close by.

Located at Rockford Green on the edge of the New Forest this welcoming inn is very popular with families. There are two large bars. Heated by an open fire the smaller of the two is mostly occupied by locals whilst the other has a servery and sunny terrace overlooking the very large garden and play area.

Owned by Gales of Horndean this well managed inn has a selection of real ales, which include Alice Lisle Bitter, Gales own HSB, Ringwood Best plus a guest ale and Stella, Fosters and country wines.

A superb menu, freshly prepared and cooked on the premises is served every day 12 – 2.15 and 5.30 – 11. On the menu are a selection of baguettes, ploughman's and salads plus 'lite bites' like Camembert wedges, deep fried and served with cranberry sauce. Also available favourites like steak & kidney, BBQ ribs, sliced ham, egg and chips, chef's special curry and chicken, bacon and leek in a creamy leek sauce topped with short crust pastry. Vegetarians are catered for with dishes such as penne pasta with tomato, olive and pesto with salad and broccoli and Stilton bake. Specials might include lobster sausages and honey roast breast of duck.

Children very welcome, dogs in pub but not in garden.

Weekday opening times 11 – 2.30 and 5.30 – 11, Saturday 11 – 3 and 6 – 11, Sunday 12 – 3 and 6 -10.30. All day opening during summer holidays.

Breamore, nr. Fordingbridge. Tel: 01725 512252. Fax: 510980
e-mail: amanda@thebatandball.com

Nestling on the edge of the New Forest, the Bat and Ball lies half way between Salisbury and Bournemouth in the delightful village of Breamore with its many thatched cottages. Just up the road is Breamore House and Countryside Museum.

Originally built some 250 years ago the Bat and Ball has for years been a popular local especially with fisherman as the pub has two miles of prime fishing on the nearby banks of the River Avon. Free to residents the stretch runs from the two bridges, at The Shallows by Breamore Mill downstream to Castle Hill. A national rod licence is all that is required, which can be purchased from the nearby village shop. There is an extensive beer garden.

The spacious through bar of this tenanted freehouse is heated by an open fire and there is a separate restaurant. Real ales presently on offer include Ringwood Best, Bass, Gales, Boddingtons and 6X.

A full snack menu is always available 11 - 2.30 (Sunday 12 - 3) and 7 - 9.30 plus daily specials such as Barberry duck breast, pan fried pheasant and lamb tagine. On the menu starters range from Thai crab cakes with a sweet chilli dip to wild mushroom risotto with shaved Parmesan. Main courses range from a seared tuna steak with lime and coriander salsa and pan fried chicken breast with creamy tarragon sauce, mashed potato and broccoli to a Mediterranean vegetable Wellington served with tomato coulis, rice and salad. There is separate children's menu and a breakfast for fishermen.

Children welcome in restaurant dogs welcome in pub and garden.

Opening times 11 – 3 and 6 – 11 Sunday 12 – 3 and 7 - 10.30.

Seven letting rooms.

CROWN INN 3

High Street, Fordingbridge. Tel : 01425 652552.

A relaxed atmosphere prevails throughout this former 17th century cream and green painted coaching inn. Upon entering the main bar one is immediately greeted by a warm roaring log fire set in the large inglenook fireplace with comfortable seating all around. There is a small dining area to the left and a pool table in an area behind the fireplace. The décor is mainly cream and white.

The pub has been run by the same licensees for over 20 years a big plus today. Real ales featured are Ringwood Best and Flowers Original plus Guinness, Murphy's, Heineken, Stella and Strongbow cider.

Food is available every day with an á la carte menu from Tuesday – Saturday. Listed on the menu is a range of sandwiches and ploughman's plus garlic bread, homemade soup, pate and prawn cocktail. Hot meals include bacon and egg toastie, various grills with chips, steak and kidney pudding, beef curry and a hot chilli Mexican. There is a choice of salads and a good range of pizzas. You are invited to create your own with additional toppings listed. A traditional roast lunch is served on Sunday.

The Crown is open all day 11 – 11 with normal Sunday hours.

En-suite overnight accommodation is available all rooms with colour TV and tea and coffee making facilities.

Winsor Road, Winsor. Nr. Cadnam. Tel: 02380 812237.

Estimated to be about 300 years old, the Compass Inn is a real pub that serves food not a restaurant where you can drink. Tucked away in the tiny village of Winsor just outside the Forest boundary it has not really changed over the years. It is a most welcoming pub, unspoilt and unpretentious with low beams and a real fire creating a cosy atmosphere. Being off the main routes far removed from the tourist trap it attracts a local crowd. The inn has won many awards including being featured in the New Forest Magazine as one of the great pub gardens due to the profusion of colour during the summer.

The Compass, run by Mop and Sophie Draper, is renowned for the splendid regularly changing real ales, which include Ringwood Bitter, Gales HSB, London Pride, Thwaites and Wadworth 6X.

Generously portioned meals, available everyday 12 – 2.30 and 6.30 – 9 include mixed grill, rib eye steak, steak and kidney pie, faggots, chips and peas, bacon hock plus doorstep sandwiches and bacon 'butties' at lunchtime.

Speciality nights are Monday for curry and Tuesday British beef night, for T-bones and 16oz rumps. The public bar has a pool table and juke box and Irish nights are held on the 1st and 3rd Thursday of each month. Beer festivals are held twice a year.

Well behaved children and dogs welcome.

The inn is open all day every day 11 – 11, Sunday 12 – 10.30.

8 ✓ THE CROWN — BRANSGORE

SMUGGLERS INN — MILFORD.

HARE & HOUNDS — SWAY

RISING SUN — WOOTEN

7 ✓ ROYAL OAK — BANK (or Hyldhurst Ale)

ITALIAN — LYNDHURST & CHRISTCHURCH (Hydroalic)
TUCKTON BRIDGE view on river.
PRETTO

CONCRETOR — LYNDHURST Rd

WOODPARK — SOPLEY

BOAT HOUSE — CHRISTCHURCH

8 ✓ THE WALTHAM ARMS — NR LYMINGTON (CARVERY)

9 ✓ THE THREE TUNS

Hamptworth, nr. Landford, Salisbury. Tel/Fax: 01794 390302.

Happily within the confines of the Forest there are still a few unspoilt inns, one of my favourites, and that of many others is the lovely thatched Cuckoo. Built some three hundred years ago it was once the village shop before becoming a pub in the 1930s. Inside one bar serves a series of small, simply furnished cosy rooms heated by open fires. Outside there are picnic benches on the front lawn with more on the sheltered side and rear terraces.

The inn is a freehouse which has just recently changed hands; happily the new licensees intend keeping the pub exactly as it is. A large selection of well kept real ales is always available which usually include Hop Back Summer Lightning and GFB, Ringwood Best, Hall & Woodhouse Tanglefoot, Wadworth 6X, and Pots Ale from the Cheriton brewhouse plus guests.

The menu available 12 – 2 (Saturday 2.30, Sunday 3) and 5.30 – 8, but not Sunday evening includes various light snacks and a small seasonal menu.

Small gatherings can be catered for and there is also a pentanque pitch available for parties.

Children and dogs in garden only.

Opening times 11.30 – 2.30 and 5.30 – 11, Saturday 11.30 – 3 and 5.30 – 11, Sunday 12 – 3.30 and 5.30 – 10.30.

Pilley, nr. Lymington. Tel: 01590 672158

One of the most attractive and oldest inns in the Forest, the Fleur De Lys is a particular favourite of mine. In the pub is a list of all the landlords since 1498 although beer is believed to have been sold here since 1096. Originally the inn was a pair of forester's cottages, the tree roots and fireplace opening (an old Forest tradition) can still be seen in the stone flagged entrance passage. The inn was described in Sir Arthur Conan Doyle's book ' The White Company' and the two bars are named after characters from the book ' The Children of the New Forest' which was written in the locality. The heavily beamed main bar has an enormous inglenook fireplace where hams were regularly smoked. There is a separate dining area and family room also a pretty rear garden.

The landlord Neil Rogers keeps a well stocked bar which includes a selection of real ales, still served traditionally straight from the barrel. They presently include Flowers Original, Gales HSB, and Ringwood Best Bitter also on tap are Heineken and Stella.

Food here is excellent the menu chalked daily on the blackboard and available 12 – 2 and 6.30 – 9.30, Sunday 12 – 2.30 and 7.30 – 9 lists dishes such as special game bangers with a fruit, bacon and Port gravy, swordfish steak marinated in chilli and apricot served on rice and a vegetarian shepherds pie. Roasted hock heads a list of traditional favourites followed by steak, kidney and Guinness pie, its 'Fleur' chilli and half a shoulder of lamb roasted 'til it falls off the bone.

Dogs on leads, children in family room.

Opening times 11 – 2.30 and 6 – 11, Sunday 12 – 3 and 7 – 10.30.

Frogham, Fordingbridge. Tel: 01425 652294, Fax: 653213

Built around the turn of the century, the Foresters Arms is a popular pub with a good local trade situated in a remote spot close to open forest evidence by the fact that one usually has to nudge ones way past donkeys who regularly congregate by the front gate. Recently renovated the main bar, heated by an open log fire, is finished in a warm red décor whilst furnishings consist of solid wood tables, chairs and pew seats. There is a separate, comfortable no-smoking dining room and a large beer garden which includes an excellent children's play area.

Well managed by Michael & Venessa Harding this Wadworth pub can offer a good choice of drinks which include their own 6X, Farmers Glory, Old Timer and IPA plus Bass and other guest ales together with Henry's Smooth, Stella, Murphy's, Heineken and Carlsberg also a small wine list.

Food is available weekdays 12 - 2.30 and 6 - 9, Saturday 12 – 3 and 6 - 9.30 Sunday lunchtime only 12 – 2.30. The specials are listed daily on the blackboard and might include carrot and coriander soup, chicken liver pate, grilled sardines and moules marinier followed by pork and smoked bacon sausages, chef's game pie, Cumberland sausage ring and a curry. The printed menu lists an open Spanish omelette, potato wedges, hot mozzarella melts and prawns in filo pastry plus favourites like ham and eggs and sausage and mash. Sweets include sticky toffee pudding, spotted dick, sherry trifle and bread and butter pudding.

Children and dogs are both equally welcome inside and out.

Weekday opening times 11 – 3 and 6 – 11, Sunday 12 - 3 and 7 – 10.30.

GLENEAGLES 8

Butts Ash Lane, Dibden Purlieu. Tel: 02380 842162.

When part of Strong & Co the Romsey brewery, which was taken over by Whitbread, the pub was known as the Jester but renamed in 1986. The interior, warmed by an open fire is adorned with golfing memorabilia collected over the years by the licensee Geoff Mercer.

A good range of drinks cater for the local trade, real ales like Strong's Best Bitter which was resurrected in 1999 and brewed by the Hampshire Brewery to the old Romsey brewers original recipe. There are also Ringwood ales, Wadworth 6X and Gales HSB.

Food is available 12 – 2.30 and 6 – 9, Saturday and Sunday 12 – 9. Apart from the usual pub snacks like jacket potatoes there is a choice of starters, vegetarian dishes, toasted torpedos, steaks and grills, Sunday roast and a very reasonable OAP menu. Daily blackboard specials might include beef curry, a 16oz-battered cod, garlic chicken and ribeye steak. Friday night is pasta night. There is a reasonably priced children's menu plus birthday parties can be arranged with a free cake for numbers of ten or more.

Only guide dogs in the pub others on a lead in the garden. Children only in the family room. Licensed music Thursday night

Weekday opening times 11 – 3 and 6 –11, Sunday 12 – 3 and 7 – 10.30.

HAPPY CHEESE 9

189 Lyndhurst Road, Ashurst. Tel: 02380 294901.

Originally built as a restaurant, the Happy Cheese is today a very nice comfortable pub attractively painted in green and cream. Wood is very much in evidence in the mostly open plan attractive beamed interior, which has a mix of tables and chairs on a part wood, and part flag-stoned floor. There is a massive fireplace with open log fire plus several cosy seating areas. Picnic benches outside on the lawn.

The pub is a Vintage Inn offering a good selection or drinks, which include Bass and Tetley Bitter real ales plus Carlsberg Export etc.

The lunch menu, commencing at 12 offers sandwiches and snacks like fresh soup, the pub's own Caesar salad, ham and mushroom melt and breaded mushroom boats. Larger plates listed include three shires sausage and Cheddar mash, creamy garlic chicken, beef, mushroom and Bass-ale pie, open chicken, leek and ham pie, ratatouille and swaddled sausage with lambs liver. A wider choice of evening meals, served until 10 p.m. include lamb Henry - a shoulder cut, braised in a root vegetable and pearl barley sauce and topped with deep fried onion strips and hunter's chicken - butterfly breast with bacon, barbecue sauce and melted cheese, with Cheddar mash and fresh vegetables.

Families in the non-smoking room. No dogs.

Weekday opening times all day 11 – 11, Sunday 12 – 10.30.

14

Durnstown, Sway. Tel: 01590 682404.

Festooned with flowers and hanging baskets, this attractive two-storey pub was originally a mortuary some 300 years ago. It occupies a lovely position on the edge of open Forest with fields to the rear. Last renovated in 1995 the interior is both warm and welcoming with a real open fire. A piano greets you as you enter the front door, on the left is a smart part panelled room and beyond a cosy dining room with an impressive fireplace, the bar is at the other end. An assortment of furniture consists of comfortable armchairs, pew seats, settles and a mix of tables and chairs. Nautical regalia is displayed around the walls together with old photographs. There is one fruit machine. Outside picnic benches are neatly positioned on the sunny front terrace with more on the grass at the rear together with a good children's play area.

Ian and his daughter Fiona are the tenants and can offer a good range of drinks including Heineken, Stella and real ales like Ringwood, 6X and Brakespear Special.

Food is served daily from 12 – 9.30 (9 Sunday). In addition to daily specials such as lambs liver and crispy bacon, marinated braised lamb shank, roast supreme of salmon and poached red bream the extensive menu also lists the usual ploughman's, baguettes and sandwiches. There is a good range of starters plus dishes like Caesar salad and a fresh mushroom pot. Also included are four vegetarian main courses, a fish selection plus homemade dishes like steak and kidney pie, sweet and sour chicken, beef lasagne, chicken curry and chilli.

Children are welcome and have their own menu. Dogs welcome inside and out. Opening times 11 – 11 Sunday 12 – 10.30.

Meeting House Lane, The Furlong, Ringwood. Tel: 01425 475139.

Owned by Ringwood Brewery this was the second of their four pubs. In the very warm and welcoming interior there are cosy rooms to the left and right of the entrance hall with open log fires, a larger bar at the back again with an open fireplace and a very attractive dark wood conservatory. Décor is rustic, part brick and part painted walls above wood panelling, the floor is mainly carpeted with an area of flagstones by the solid brick built bar. Ringwood Brewery organises weekday trips round the brewery followed by a ploughman's at the pub. Details usually pinned on the wall.

The full range of Ringwood's ales is available which include their Best Bitter, Fortyniner, the award winning Old Thumper and winter Porter. In addition there is Kronenberg, Konig, Stonehouse cider and Thatchers plus Ringwood's own red and white wine.

Food is served every lunchtime 12 - 2.30 and available in the bars or in a separate conservatory. Blackboard specials might include traditional favourites such as chilli con carne, liver and bacon and a chicken curry whilst the set menu lists ham, egg and fries and fish, chips and peas. Snacks include ploughman's, omelettes, beef burgers, pork and leek sausages with crusty bread and sandwiches – plain and toasted.

Various events include live music nights.

Children and dogs are equally welcome.

Opening times all day 11 – 11, Sunday 12 – 11.

Quay Hill, Lymington. Tel: 01590 672709, Fax: 688453.

Located at the top of the picturesque cobbled Quay Hill, the Kings Head dates back to 1836 prior to which it was a baker's shop. The very atmospheric interior has a wealth of beams, wood panelling beneath bare brick and painted walls, bare wood floors throughout, an interesting mix of furnishings, a wood burning stove in a brick fireplace and a large open fireplace at the far end. The pub is beautifully kept with many interesting artefacts including beer mugs hanging from the beams. There is a small patio at the rear.

Real ales presently available are Gales HSB, Old Speckled Hen, Ringwood True Glory, Fullers London Pride and Flowers Original.

Meals can be selected from two menus. Available 12 – 2 & 6 – 10, there is a choice of starters and 'light bites' like garlic sautéed king prawns and chicken strips with a spring onion salad plus sandwiches and jacket potatoes. Main courses include roasted half shoulder of lamb, chicken and spring onion stir fry, roasted red pepper and Stilton tart and C.O.D... calories on demand a Kings Head favourite with local sausages, potatoes, onions, tomatoes, mushrooms and a secret ingredient. The specials menu ranges from calamari with a spicy dip and ostrich with cherry tomatoes and mushrooms to a dressed crab with salad and granary bread and venison steak red wine and mushrooms.

Children and dogs welcome.

Opening times 11 – 2.30 and 6 – 11. Normal Sunday hours.

Beaulieu. Tel: 01590 612324 Fax: 612188. e-mail: enquires@montaguarms.co.uk

Recently re-named Monty's, this popular drinking establishment adjoins the charming Montagu Arms Hotel, one of the best in the area. It is close to Lord Montagu's National Motor Museum and at the start of a picturesque walk to Bucklers Hard described in Mike Power's book 'Pub Walks in Hampshire'. Whilst Monty's caters for its local clientele, the wooden panelling and soft furnishings give way to a more formal atmosphere. The bar is nevertheless comfortably furnished with an open fire.

Real ale choice includes Flower's Original, Ringwood and Boddington's Bitter. Also Whitbread Best, Heineken, Stella Artois, Thatchers and dry Blackthorn cider.

Monty's has a menu to suit all types of palate offering 'lite bites' and sandwiches plus intricate dishes like confit of duckling, apple compote and Madeira jus with vegetables, rump of lamb, herb mash, minted gravy and vegetables, chargrilled rib eye of beef, black pepper, cream, mushrooms and tomato and skate wing with capers, shallots and parsley black butter all cooked to perfection with excellent service. In addition there are dishes for vegetarians like braised leek and filo pastry parcel with a cream and white wine sauce, a children's menu, pasta meals and freshly prepared salads. Usual times are 12 – 2.30 and 6 – 9, weekends 12 – 3 and 6 – 9.30 but generally all day in high season.

Children welcome, dogs in one half of bar only.

Weekday opening times 10 – 3 and 6 – 11, Saturday 10 – 11, Sunday 10 - 10.30.

Accommodation is available in the hotel next door.

Romsey Road, Ower. Tel: 02380 814379. e-mail: mortimershq@btinternet.com

Known previously as Mortimer's Tavern the Mortimer Arms Hotel is situated just off the M27 at junction 2 almost on the doorstep to Paulton's Park - a family leisure park with many rides and exotic birds. Once a fine residence the Mortimer Arms Hotel is today a very attractive and beautifully kept pub, The interior is mostly open plan with a wooden floor by the attractive bar, carpeted elsewhere. Furniture is in keeping with the age of the pub well polished solid upholstered wooden chairs and sturdy tables. There is a dining area to the rear with seats on the grass and outside terrace.

Paul Wilson is the licensee of this freehouse offering four real ales, Ringwood Best, Romsey IPA, Wadworth 6X plus a guest such as Hop Back Summer Lightning

Apart from the usual snacks such as sandwiches and baguettes there is set menu and specials chalked daily on the blackboard. Available everyday of the week from 12 – 2.30 and 7 – 9.30, the imaginative list of starters might include deep fried Cajun sardines, potted kipper pate with a taramasalata dip, camembert fritters with cayenne pepper, tomato mozzarella and basil vinaigrette and baked eggs with smoke salmon cheese. Also on the main menu there are tempting dishes like roasted duck breast with French chestnut honey and crushed peppercorn deglazed with Madeira wine, roast rack of local lamb with shallots and pesto crust and breaded chicken breast with Dorset smoked Stilton and field mushrooms. Lovers of shellfish might choose crab cakes with Cajun scallops and king prawns whilst vegetarians might prefer butter bean and Cheddar hash with tomato salsa. An interesting hot salad has blackened crispy duck noodles with broccoli florets, wild rice and orange plum vinaigrette.

Children welcome, dogs in garden only.

The hotel is open everyday of the week 11 - 11

4 en-suite rooms.

Emery Down, Lyndhurst. Tel: 01703 282329

The New Forest Inn is delightfully situated in the heart of the New Forest on the edge of this pretty hamlet. The area is a popular destination for Forest visitors and the New Forest ponies which congregate around the pub, enhancing the pub's charm. The land was claimed from the king by squatters in the 1700's and became the site of a caravan trader who sold groceries and ales. The caravan now forms the front lounge and part of the bar. Enlarged over the years this attractive Forest inn offers the modern traveller a warm welcome in a relaxed atmosphere. Part panelled walls, beamed ceilings and assorted furnishings characterise the open plan bar with comfortable alcoves and decorated with Forest bric-a-brac. Throughout the summer months a picturesque garden can be found at the rear of the pub.

This managed inn, once owned by Whitbread, sells a range of real ales and fine stouts as well as Heineken, Stella and a fine selection of fine wines sold by the bottle or glass.

The inn is noted for its home-cooked New Forest dishes and fresh fish served all week 12 – 9.30 (9 Sunday).

Dogs and children are welcome inside.

Weekday opening times all day 11 – 11, Sunday 12 – 10.30.

4 en-suite bed & breakfast rooms.

Inn featured in Egon Ronay's Pub & Inns and is recommended by Les Routiers.

Ibsley, nr Ringwood. Tel: 01425 473387.

Originally three 14th- century worker's cottages on the Somerley estate the Old Beams is a very attractive, two-story thatched inn on the main Ringwood to Fordingbridge road very close to the River Avon. The front porch leads directly into a small atmospheric room heated by an open coal fire beyond which is the large open plan dining area, which extends in summer to a conservatory and the garden beyond.

Manager's wine selection includes two Australian reds and one white plus Venture Cove sauvignon a highly recommend white from New Zealand. Real ales presently listed are Courage Best, Theakston's Old Peculiar and XB also Beamish Black and a range of lagers. Tea and coffee also available.

Food is available daily 12 – 2.15 and 6 – 9 with a minimum advertised wait of 20 minutes. To start with there is chef's homemade soup, garlic mushrooms, smoked salmon and dill and spanakopitta – spinach and Feta cheese mixed with herbs and spices and encased in filo and served with a cheese dip. A range of old English fayre includes beef Wellington, liver and bacon, steak and ale pie, steak and kidney pudding, mignons of lamb and New Forest game pie. Pasta dishes range from lasagne bologna and Mediterranean pasta bake to mushroom tortellini and chicken pasta. There is a range of grills and fish dishes like tempura battered snapper, a duo of smoked haddock and Mozzarella fish cakes and deep fried lemon pepper breaded scallops. Separate children's menu and daily specials.

Families welcome but no dogs.

Opening times 11.30 – 3 and 6 – 11, normal Sunday hours.

Lime Kiln Lane, Holbury. Tel: 02380 891137 e-mail: oldmillinnnewforest.co.uk

Peacefully located in a valley at the bottom of a track beside open Forest yet only minutes from Fawley is the very atmospheric Old Mill Inn. Part of the bar was originally the miller's cottage dating back to the 12th century whilst the large high-beamed restaurant is a Queen Ann barn brought in from Hartley Witney in 1976. Exploring the rest of the interior one finds high and low beamed ceilings, discreet alcoves, cosy corners and a large inglenook fireplace with a warm log fire on cold winter days. The front is mainly lawn with a pond, picnic benches and an extremely large children's play area.

The pub is a freehouse personally run by the owner who took over at the end of 2000. A good range of drinks include several real ales like Ringwood Old Thumper and Fortyniner.

Lunch is served daily from 12 – 2 and every evening from 7. Speaking to the landlord he tells me that all the beef sold here is maize and grass fed, the lamb down and pasture fed, the pork cider and apple fed and all the chickens reared on GM free feed. From the menu one has a choice of starters like homemade soup, mushroom hotchpotch and cheese and prawn garlic bread. Fish dishes range form pan-fried cod in a lemon sauce to Cajun salmon supreme. Other main meals include steamed rabbit pudding, a mixed game cassoulet, duck breast stir fry, pork cooked in cider and Stilton and a warm chicken and bacon salad. Vegetarians can choose between mushroom stroganoff, Oriental stir-fried vegetables and a home-made vegetable curry. In addition there are daily specials and a traditional Sunday roast.

Dogs and children welcome

Friday, Saturday and Sunday the inn is open all day from 11 with happy hour between 3 and 5 on Friday. The rest of the week 11 – 2.30 and 5 – 11.

Three beautiful en-suite rooms, tastefully furnished with all facilities. Accommodation for caravans and campers.

ORIGINAL WHITE HART   18

Market Place, Ringwood. Tel: 01425 472702. Fax: 471993.

This popular inn sign is believed to date back from the time of Henry VII who was hunting in the New Forest with Archduke Philip of Spain and his wife Joan pursuing a magnificent stag. Having cornered the creature Joan asked that its life be spared after which they repaired to the inn for refreshment. The inn was subsequently re-named.

This old coaching inn was totally refurbished in 1999 all work being sympathetically carried out. Upon entering the part carpeted and wooden floored front bar you are greeted by a warm log fire in the large inglenook fireplace. There is another seating area on the left with a fireplace and an attractive blue painted dining room on the right with an interesting cast iron fireplace. The bar extends to the rear where comfortable arm chairs allow you to relax a while before entering the large airy restaurant.

Owned by Eldridge Pope the range of real ales include Hardy Country plus a guest beer such as Bass.

The menu, available all day lists a comprehensive choice of starters available in large or small portions, like steamed Bantry Bay mussels finished with white wine and cream and home-cooked roast duck nestled on Caesar salad with shaved Parmesan. Main dishes range from monkfish and salmon fillet rolled in Cajun spices and sat on a lake of tomato and cream fish sauce and a sizzling skillet to a crisp crumb rack of lamb and a vegetable jambalaya.

Children welcome, dogs in bar only

Weekday opening times all day 10 – 11, Sunday 12 – 10.30.

Accommodation in single, double and family rooms. Four poster bed extra.

ROSE & CROWN   19

Lyndhurst Road, Brockenhurst. Tel: 01590 622225. Fax: 623056.

The present house dates from the 18th century and enjoys commoner's rights to cords of firewood and the grazing of up to six ponies in the Forest. The lounge and Forest Bar are comfortably furnished heated by a warm open fire.

Real ales on offer include Hardy Country, Courage Directors and Courage Best Bitter plus Eldridge Pope Smooth, Fosters and Kronenberg 1664.

An informal dining system operates during the summer with a partial waitress service during spring, autumn and winter. Food times are generally from 12 – 2 but can be longer in summer; 6-9 Monday-Thursday, 6 – 9.30 Friday and Saturday. Apart from snacks such as sandwiches, ploughman's and jacket potatoes, potato wedges are listed on the menu together with garlic mushrooms. Smokey Joe is a chicken breast topped with BBQ sauce, bacon and melted cheese whilst 'surf and turf sizzler' is a 10 oz rump steak with king prawns sautéed in garlic butter and served on a sizzling platter. Old favourites include steak and kidney pie, cottage pie, gammon pork and ale sausage served in a giant Yorkshire pudding and a giant mixed grill.

Children and dogs welcome.

Opening times all day 11 – 11 Sunday 12 – 10.30.

14 en-suite rooms with SKY TV, trousers press, tea and coffee making facilities etc.

Rockbourne, Fordingbridge. Tel: 01725 518236.
e-mail: enquires@roseandthistle.co.uk

Rockbourne is one of the loveliest villages in Hampshire. Situated amid rolling downland a small brook runs the entire length of the winding main street passing some idyllic thatched cottages and handsome period houses. Situated at the northern end is the charming thatched Rose & Thistle. Originally two cottages it became an inn almost 200 years ago. Inside the bar, divided by timber props, features an open fire and a mix of old pine, oak settles, tables and chairs on the flag stone floor. A massive inglenook fireplace housing a warm log fire in winter dominates the restaurant. The front garden has a terrace with attractive cast-iron and wooden tables with benches and tables on the lawn.

The inn is a freehouse well run by the owner Tim Norfolk for the past 7 years. Guest ales are alongside Fullers London Pride and a selection from Adnams.

An interesting menu is available every day 12 – 2.30 and 7 – 9.30. Sunday evening only from April to October. Heading the list of light lunch homemade favourites is a warm goats cheese and bacon salad, scrambled eggs with smoked salmon and prawns and an elegant Welsh rarebit with bacon and tomato. To follow pork fillet stuffed with apricots and pistachio nuts, roast rack of lamb, supreme of chicken and a pie or casserole. The dinner menu is similar with the addition of chateaubriand for two and Gressingham duck breast served on spinach with an apricot sauce. Vegetarians can choose between a vegetable stir fry with a mixture of nuts and a herb and garlic tagliatelle with julienne of vegetables in tomatoes. Daily fish dishes are listed on the blackboard.

Dogs in garden only, children welcome.

Weekday opening times 11 - 3 and 6 - 11, Sunday 12 - 3 and 7 - 10.30.

Ringwood Road, North Gorley, Fordingbridge. Tel: 01425 652244

Recently renovated and re-thatched this idyllically located, picturesque 17th century pub occupies a peaceful position overlooking a duck pond. The front porch leads directly into the non-smoking Kings Bar, which has a low boarded ceiling, comfortably furnished and heated by an open log fire. Adjoining, the larger extended Cromwell Bar has a heavily beamed ceiling, part carpeted floor and assorted furnishings with an attractive corner brick fireplace housing a warm wood burning stove. Down one step and you enter a family room with a cosy seating area which doubles as a half size skittle alley. There is seating at the front and picnic benches on the rear lawn. The Royal Oak is a popular meeting venue being the headquarters of Hyde Cricket Club and The Royal Oak Racing Syndicate.

Well run by the licensees a good range of well kept beers include Flowers Best, Ringwood Bitter and a guest ale plus Murphy's, Guinness and a range of lagers. Freshly made tea and coffee is available all times.

Very good homemade food is available 12 – 2.30 and 6.30 – 9. Specials such as a celery and bean chilli, lasagne, curry and steak, kidney and ale pie supplement the printed menu which includes snacks and starters like soup and deep fried chicken or vegetable samosas plus toasted sandwiches and ploughman's. There is freshly grilled fish, steaks, New Forest mixed grill, traditional ham and eggs and gammon steak. Most meals are available as half portions. Children have their own menu and vegetarians are catered for.

Children welcome in the family room and dogs on a lead.

Weekday opening times all day 11 - 11, Sunday 12 - 10.30.

The Quay, Lymington. Tel: 01590 676903.

Lymington is a maritime town very popular with sailors and having a very good climate generally with more sunny days than towns further inland. There is a small car park in front of the Ship and a public parking area the other side of the slip.

Latitude 50 45/52 north, Longitude 132/14 west translated in layman's terms is the position of the Ship according to the sign outside. Occupying an idyllic position the inn is positioned right on the quay at Lymington at the bottom of a picturesque cobbled street with views across the Lymington River and its marinas.

The inn is a Brewers Fayre pub having a mostly open plan interior, the front of which is mainly bar area whilst the rear is mostly for dining. On the left hand wall is a handsome wooden fire surround featuring a built-in clock.

Real ales on offer include Flowers Original and Boddingtons Bitter. Also Whitbread Best, Heineken Export, Stella Artois, Caffreys and Strongbow cider.

Food is available all day the menu being the standard Brewers Fayre. Typical starters range from potato skins to the ultimate combo – chicken goujons, scampi, garlic breaded mushrooms, battered onion rings, garlic bread, potato wedges and a selection of three dips. There are the usual steaks and grills plus traditional favourites which include drunken duck – diced lamb with onions and mushrooms in a red currant, port and red wine sauce.

Children welcome but no dogs.

Opening times all day 11 – 11, Sunday 12 – 10.30.

Old Romsey Road, Cadnam Tel: 02380 812236

Tucked beneath the end of the motorway the Sir John Barleycorn is reached from exit 1 of the M27 at the entrance to the New Forest. It is a long, low thatched inn dating back to the 12th century and believed to be one of the oldest in Hampshire. Originally cottages one of which belonged to Purkiss the woodcutter who it is said found the body of King Rufus. The very atmospheric interior consists of three main carpeted bar areas and a large smart restaurant, Furnishings consist of assorted tables, chairs and benches. The lower bar has a heavily beamed ceiling, dark wood furnishings and heated by a large open log fire whilst a thatched servery is a feature in the higher bar together with hops suspended from the ceiling and many old interesting photographs and artefacts on the walls. Tables and benches are neatly positioned at the front to make the most of the sunny position.

The inn is a Wayside Inn. Real ales presently include Flower's Original, Ringwood Best and True Glory also Stella, Heineken, Strongbow and Guinness.

Blackboard specials such as battered cod, gunpowder pork – loin in a cream, peppercorn and mustard sauce, fish pie, half a roast chicken and lambs liver and bacon also dishes like steak and mushroom suet pudding, steak Diane, lemon sole, rainbow trout supplement the set menu which includes typical pub fayre. Food is available all day 11.30 - 9.30ish.

Families in restaurant. Only guide dogs allowed inside

The inn is open all day every day 11 – 11, Sunday 12 – 10.30.

Canterton, nr. Cadnam. Tel: 02380 813170.

Popular with tourists, this interesting pub occupying a sunny position overlooking open Forest is named, it is said after the alleged assassin of King William, nick-named Rufus after his long red hair. Nearby Rufus Stone, a monument erected in 1745 but later covered with an iron protector, marks the spot where on August 2 1100 he is reputed to have met his death whilst hunting.

A series of open plan rooms, with assorted chairs, tables and padded wall bench-es, radiate from the central bar whilst lots of interesting paraphernalia adorns the walls and ceilings. There is a very attractive dining room and a cool summer patio overlooking the garden where there are excellent facilities for children of all ages.

The pub is owned by Surrey Inns and has a well stocked bar which includes four real ales, No Name Bitter, Wadworth 6X , Courage Directors and Courage Best.

Food, served daily 12 – 2 and 6 – 9 (Sunday 8), can be chosen from a series of small blackboards. A typical selection might include Hawaiian platter, large bat-tered cod, steamed queen fish, with Oriental vegetables and crackers, red peppers, spinach and mushroom lasagne, Thai vegetable schnitzel, steak ale and mushroom pie, sliced ham with mustard sauce, Directors's sausage and mash and pink pep-percorn char-grilled garlic and herb chicken. For heartier appetites there is the Tyrrell mega grill plus a full rack of hickory ribs. Traditional sweets range from spotted dick to rhubarb crumble and custard. Also the usual snacks like jacket potatoes and ploughman's and a separate children's menu.

The pub is a family pub and welcomes children and there is no objection to dogs on a lead in the pub but not the rear garden.

Opening times 11 - 3 and 6 -11.30, Saturday and Sunday all day from 11.

Station Road, Fordingbridge. Tel: 01425 652098.
e-mail: peter@augustusjohn.fordingbridge.com

Located a mile from Fordingbridge on the Damerham road this pub has undergone two name changes in the past 25 years. Originally the Railway Hotel it became the Load of Hay before resulting in the present name. With the name change came complete refurbishment and it is now a very comfortable inn heated in winter by an open fire.

Real ales include Courage Best, Hardy's Country plus Foster and Kronenberg lager.

Recommended in the Michelin Good Food Guide one can eat during the week from around 12 - 2.30 (3 on Sunday) and 7 - 9.30. There is menu offering the usual pub fayre such as ham, egg and chips, homemade lasagne, steak and kidney pie and curries. Daily specials on the board include fresh fish and meals such as Cumberland sausages with a mash and onion gravy and oven roasted duck breast with a port and ginger sauce plus three or four roasts on a Sunday.

Children and dogs are welcome.

Opening times 11 – 3 and 6.30 – 11, normal Sunday hours.

Four well appointed en-suite rooms.

Beaulieu Road, Lyndhurst. Tel: 02380 292342

Situated in an isolated position on Beaulieu Heath and close to the railway station this friendly inn, which has been offering a warm welcome to the weary traveller since 1848, has a view of open Forest and the pony sales yard next door. The original stables block is now incorporated into the tastefully refurbished bar area neatly separated from the long narrow, popular restaurant. Flagstone floors, wattle ceiling and roaring log winter fires create a warm and welcoming atmosphere, which is enhanced by a collection of heavy horse tack on the walls and hop vines that festoon the bar. Outside there is an extensive landscaped garden with a fenced-in children's play area

The inn is run by Michael Elvis, the former UK 'Innkeeper of the Year' and well known licensee in the New Forest. A wide range of real ales are available, Courage Best, Directors, Ringwood Old Thumper, Fullers London Pride and guest real ales on tap. Also on draught John Smiths Bitter, Beamish, Guinness, Fosters and Kronenberg larger and Thatcher's Cider.

The wide ranging and good value 'bar menu' includes Forest broth and crusty bread for those cold days, homemade baguettes and a selection of hot sandwiches such as char-grilled chicken with smoked Cheddar, lettuce tomato and mayonnaise or goats cheese with Provençal vegetables with basil. Also a selection of char-grilled items as well as filled jacket potatoes. A specials board is available 7 days a week together with a separate restaurant and children's menu.

The inn is mud friendly, dog friendly and even mothers-in-law are welcome too!!

Opening hours all day in summer 11 - 11, winter 11 – 3 and 6 – 11, Monday to Friday all day 11 – 11, Saturday 11 – 11, Sunday 12 – 10.30.

Brook, nr. Lyndhurst. Tel: 02380 812214. Fax: 813958
e-mail: bell@bramshaw.co.uk
AA rosette for superb food for the 8th consecutive year.

The Bell at Brook has been providing traditional New Forest hospitality since 1782. The atmosphere is friendly and the staff are polite – the sort that remember you from a previous visit. The building has many original features notably in the bar with its inglenook fireplace and antique prints of rural scenes which recall the history of the Bell as a drover's halt and hunting lodge.

The Bell has been owned by the Crosthwaite-Eyre family throughout its history, and behind the hotel under the same control is Bramshaw Golf Club (with its two 18-hole courses) and Dunwood Manor only a short drive away.

A freehouse it offers a varying selection of real ales such as Ringwood Best and Directors plus John Smith Smooth and Courage Best Bitter, plus 30 malt whiskies.

The excellent food served from 12 – 2.30 and 6 – 9.30 is noted for its range of high standard and value for money deals warranting inclusion in some of the top guides. Apart from snacks like freshly baked baguettes, Smokey Blue burgers and favourites such as drover's lunch blackboard specialities listed might include terrine of game with a tomato and onion pickle, thinly sliced breast of smoked duck served with an apricot chutney and grilled goats cheese set on to a citrus salad. Followed by fillet of sea bass with garlic, ginger and chilli, roast rump of lamb with braised red cabbage and pasta spirals with a Provençal sauce.

Children are welcome in the family room where they have their own menu.

The Bell is open all day every day.

Accommodation in 25 en-suite rooms.

Station Street, Lymington. Tel: 01590 675140.

The building dates back to the opening of the railway on July 12th 1858 when it was known as the Railway Inn and formed part of the extensive smugglers tunnel network that criss-crossed Lymington.

Lying close to the marina and harbour it is within easy reach of the Isle of Wight ferry. The spacious interior, heated by an open fire, is beautifully kept with a nautical theme throughout. A unique pergola creation of authentic Roman garden design can be found in the award-winning garden at the rear.

Well run by the landlords, Roger and Cheryl Ling, this busy Wadworth inn caters particularly well for the sailing crowd being especially busy at weekends. Real ales listed include 6X, IPA and Boddington Bitter.

Weekdays 12 – 2 and 6.30 – 10, Sunday 12 – 3 and 7 – 9 a large selection of food is available including fresh fish like shark steak with a prawn sauce and a cod fillet dressed with cream and prawn sauce. Blackboard specials might include celery, vegetable and cream of Stilton soup, chicken curry, a mini shoulder of lamb cooked in red wine, rosemary and mushroom sauce, New Forest sausages and chicken fillets in various sauces. Sweets include chocolate fudge cake, spotted dick

Dogs are welcome and children catered for with a safe enclosed garden.

Weekday opening times 11 – 3 and 6 – 11, Saturday 11 – 11, Sunday 12 – 10.30

The Bosun's Chair offers superior bed & Breakfast accommodation with en-suite rooms.

SKY sport TV in the bar.   31

The Cross, Burley. Tel: 01425 403448. Fax: 01425 402058.

This large imposing Victorian dwelling was originally a country hotel but after a change of ownership in 2000 was converted by Wadworth & Co, the Wiltshire brewers to a comfortable and welcoming inn. Inside on the left is a small room with a warm winter log fire but the main area is on the right where there is an assortment of tables and chairs even a piano where would-be pianists are invited to tinkle the ivories. Rugs on the bare wood floor add to the ambience. On the side is a long conservatory type bar with a mix of country furnishings. Ample parking at the inn also public parking in the centre of the village.

The well stocked bar includes three real ales Wadworth's own IPA and 6X plus Toms Tipple brewed locally at the Red Shoot Inn.

Food is available every day 12 – 2 and 6 – 9.30 (Sunday 9). The set menu lists 'lite bites', sandwiches, ploughman's and dishes such as local pork sausages, mash and gravy, homemade chilli, lasagne and steak & Forest ale pie. More dishes listed daily on the blackboard might include Parma ham wrapped Brie with cranberry sauce, Feta cheese and olive salad, Burley Inn style steaks, half a roast shoulder of lamb with mint gravy, mixed grill, breast of duck with orange and cranberry, lemon sole in herb butter, Provencal vegetable pie and a peppered red eye steak.

Families and dogs welcome.

Opening times 11 – 3 & 6 – 11, usual Sunday hours.

Nine en-suite rooms.

Burley Road, Bransgore. Christchurch. Tel/Fax: 01425 762295.

Pubs named after a trade generally indicated that the landlord was associated with that particular business, I'm not sure if this is the case with this pub which dates from early this century but as the bar is adorned with old carpenters tools this could certainly be a possibility. The rustic, barn-like appearance has lots of old beams heavy furnishings and cosy seating areas with an open fire. Outside is a garden with play area.

John and Lynn Houghton are the tenants of this Eldridge Pope pub presently offering a range of real ales, which include Courage Best, Hardy Country Ale, Royal Oak and Marston's Pedigree. Also available Fosters, Millers, Kronenberg, John Smiths Bitter and Blackthorn cider.

Standard pub fayre, all home-cooked to order is available Tuesday to Friday 12 – 2, Saturday 12 – 9 and Sunday 12 – 6. A varied menu lists a range of starters such as sliced smoked salmon and homemade soup followed by various steaks, grills, fried fish, scampi and chicken dishes. Vegetarians have a selection of meals as do those who just require a salad or an omelette. Tempting sweets range from toffee apple pie with cream to dream delight sundaes.

Dogs and children both equally welcome.

Weekday opening times 11. 3 and 5.30 – 11, Saturday all day 11.30 – 11.30, Sunday 12 – 10.30.

Whitsbury. Tel: 01725 518362

The very attractive cottagy Cartwheel Inn must surely be everyone's idea of the ideal country pub. Situated in peaceful Whitsbury with its racing stables, it is an area of outstanding natural beauty. Originally two cottages built in 1796 it became an inn around 1860 when it was just known as The Wheel. At that time it was supplied with beer from Carter's Brewery in Ringwood. There is one main cosy, beamed bar having bare brick and timbered walls with an open fireplace, a separate games room and a cosy candlelit dining room. Outside there is sunny raised beer garden with picnic benches and a children's slide.

The bar is well stocked with a good range of drinks including six handpumps which dispense beers like Ringwood Fortyniner and Hop Back Summer Lightning. You will also find two ciders and a wide choice of Continental bottled largers.

An extensive menu is served 12 – 2.30 and 6 – 9.30, Sunday 7 - 9. A range of snacks include sandwiches and rolls, ploughman's, jacket potatoes, egg mayonnaise and roll mop herrings followed by dishes like Coronation chicken salad, ham egg and chips and English lamb chops with tomatoes.

Dogs and families welcome.

Opening times 11 - 2.30 and 6 – 11, Sunday 12 – 3 and 7 – 10.30.

Lyndhurst Road, Hinton Admiral. Tel: 01425 276050. Fax: 282934.

For many centuries this site has offered rest to travellers. It was recorderd in the Domesday Book as a hospice 'house of St Catherine the Faithful' and run by monks of Christchurch Priory to offer shelter to New Forest travellers.

Built sometime in the 18th century this charming and much photographed pub is now a Harvester Inn and although a large dining room was added to the rear the inn retains its original charm. The main bar has an open log fire, heavily beamed ceiling with a mix of bench seats, tables and chairs on the stone and tiled floor.

The inn is well run by Steve and Anne. Their draught Bass is a big favourite together with Worthington Cream-flow and Caffreys. Also on draught is Carling Black Label, Guinness and Grolsch.

The Cat & Fiddle is open all day for food offering a reasonably priced two-course lunch which includes steak, fresh fish and vegetarian choices. From Monday – Friday between 5 and 6 the 'early bird' deal gets you an automatic one-third off the price of all adult meals. All food is spit roasted or char-grilled 'visually' so that 'a sense of theatre is present'. The free salad cart is also a huge attraction to all Harvester regular diners

There is an outside play area and facilities for disabled persons.

Families welcome and dogs in the garden only (with hygiene aware owners).

Pub opening times presently 11 – 11, Sunday all day 12 – 10.30.

35

Ridgeway Lane, Lower Woodside, Pennington. Tel: 01590 673415

This very atmospheric creeper-covered inn lies close to the sea and salt beds in a peaceful lane. Drawing clientele from far and wide it dates from the 16th century and was once the local salt exchange. It is a charming, simple yet stylish inn positively bursting with character and a popular venue for the local yachting fraternity. The warm and welcoming interior, heated by an efficient wood burning stove in winter, is simply furnished with comfortable chairs, various old tables and pews positioned on the part-tiled and part-boarded floor Outside there is a sunny courtyard with picnic benches, and a neat walled garden with terrace.

The inn is a freehouse with a good choice of real ales, which presently include Ringwood Best, Wadworth 6X and Bass plus a changing guest beer.

Excellent food is served both lunch time and every evening, the list chalked daily on the blackboard. There are the usual pub favourites like jacket potatoes, ploughman's, filled French sticks and homemade soup. Fresh fish features strongly and includes crab, lobster, whole plaice, lemon sole and trout. The menu also highlights local game and dishes such as rack of lamb, seafood lasagne, steaks, various pasta followed by a selection of homemade puddings. Separate restaurant with a comprehensive à la carte menu.

Dogs are allowed and children away from the bar

Opening times 11 – 2.30 ish and 6 – 11, sometimes all day on Saturday and Sunday.

THE COACH & HORSES   34

Southampton Road, Cadnam. Tel: 02380 813120. Fax: 02380 812565.

Attractively painted yellow and blue, the Coach & Horses is a bright and cheery pub where the licensees Brian and Andrea Morrison have an aptitude for hospitality and a flair for creating a warm and welcoming atmosphere. The entire pub is beautifully well kept. The Coachman's Bar has a beamed ceiling and a board and carpeted floor. There is a large no-smoking area and a lounge where you can relax in the comfort of sofas in front of the fire. There is a large garden with picnic benches.

The pub has a superb wine list, a selection of whiskies and a wide range of real ales which include Ringwood, London Pride and Strongs.

The pub offers traditional home-cooked food which is served all day, incorporating quick light lunches, affordable snacks, a fun kids menu, à la carte dining alongside the excellent fresh fish and specials board. There are eight starters on the printed menu ranging from vegetarian stuffed mushrooms to smoke salmon cornets and to follow various grills, a BBQ rack of ribs, fish dishes, traditional pies and puddings like steak and ale and chicken and ham plus house specialities. Braised knuckle of lamb is a large knuckle cooked with garlic and rosemary then served with red wine gravy whilst Mediterranean chicken is the breast lightly steamed nestled on a bed of roasted seasonal vegetables in a rich Mediterranean sauce. For the sweet toothed a fantastic sweet trolley is brought to the table. Vegetarians are well catered for as are those just wanting a snack.

Children and dogs are both equally welcome inside and out.

Hours all day 11 - 11, Sunday 12 – 10.30.

THE COMPASSES INN   35

Damerham, nr. Fordingbridge. Tel: 01725 518231, Fax: 518880.

Find the Compasses Inn and you have found one of the best. Dating back over 400 years the inn was at one time virtually self sufficient with its own brewery.

Owned and personally run by the Kidd family you are assured of a warm welcome. There is a cosy public bar warmed by open fires, a small lounge bar and a large comfortably furnished dining room. A central fireplace with log burner heats both rooms. There are picnic benches on the lawns plus a children's play area.

The extremely well stocked bar of this freehouse include five real ales, their own Compasses Ale, Summer Lightning, Wadworth 6X, Ringwood Best plus a guest ale. There are 51 wines listed and 120 malt whiskies choice enough for anyone.

Excellent imaginative food is available every lunch time 12 – 2.30 and evenings 7 - 9.30 (Sunday 9). Prepared from the freshest of ingredients there is a set menu where your can choose a simple ploughman's with homemade bread, pickles and chutney or freshly made sandwiches. Special dishes chalked daily on the blackboard could include cullen skink - a dish made from Finnan haddock and potatoes also chicken, black pudding and bacon parcel with red wine. Other dishes might include John Dory with watercress, orange and chives, medallions of beef with asparagus, mango and Emmental and casserole of beer braised vegetables. To follow there is a good range of sweets and some excellent cheese.

Families welcome, clean wellies, boots and dogs allowed in public bar

Opening times 11 - 3 and 6 - 11, Saturday all day 11 - 11, Sunday 12 – 3.30 and 7 - 11.

6 en-suite rooms (one family room and four-poster).

Clay Hill, Lyndhurst. Tel/Fax: 02380 282272. e-mail: tbar@supernet.com

The Crown and Stirrup, which dates from the 15th century, is situated a little way out from Lyndhurst on the Brockenhurst road. The interesting name relates to Tudor times when the King and his entourage hunted in the Forest. Commoners could only hunt if their dogs were small enough to pass through the 'Verderer's Stirrup' which can still be seen today hanging in the Verderer's Hall in Queen's House, Lyndhurst, a former Royal Hunting Lodge.

Originally two small rooms, the last refurbishment was carried out as recently as 2001 creating more room at the back. There are lots of exposed beams, comfortable furniture and a brick fireplace with open fires.

The well stocked bar presently includes four regularly changing guest real ales plus three lagers, Guinness, Caffreys, 'Boddies' and cider.

Food all home cooked is available 12 – 2.30 and 6- 9.30 seven days a week. Available at lunchtime only are the usual snacks of soup, ploughman's, filled baguettes and jacket potatoes with a choice of six fillings. A vast specials board which includes exotic meals like wild boar, ostrich, kangaroo and crocodile supplements the main menu listing several starters followed by a mixed grill, Cajun chicken breast, lemon sole, minted lamb steak in a rich red wine sauce and a trio of sausages with parsley mash and caramelised gravy. Vegetarians have a choice of dishes like sweet and sour stir-fry on a bed of rice. Sunday roasts are available, sometimes all day. Curry nights and theme nights.

Children welcome, dogs only on a lead.

Opening times all day 11 – 11, Sunday 12 – 10.30.

V. Gd but a bit expen

Old Christchurch Road, Everton, Lymington. Tel: 01590 642655. Fax: 641370

Tucked off the main Lymington to Christchurch road, the Crown is a typical village local with a history dating back some 500 years. It was originally known as the Yeovilton Post House named after the village at that time. It meant evil town, a name associating the village with witchcraft where it was said a horse died eating the foliage.

The comfortable, beamed lounge bar is heated by an open fire there is also a separate public bar.

Peter and Phillippa Roberts are the present tenants offering Ringwood Best Bitter and Strong's Country plus an extensive wine menu and a fine selection of Scotch whiskies and liqueurs.

An interesting menu, available 11.30 – 2.30 and 6.30 – 9.30, Sunday 12 – 2.30 and 7 – 9, includes a wide selection of fish, shellfish and game. Speciality dishes include roast rack of lamb with a herb crust and goats cheese sauce perfumed with garden rosemary, roast monkfish wrapped in smoked bacon with a Muscat wine and peppercorn sauce, roast breast of pheasant, with a juniper and cranberry essence and medallions of fillet steak with wild woodland mushrooms finished with Scotch whisky.

Children welcome, dogs in garden only.

Weekday opening times 11 – 3 and 6 – 11, Sunday 12 – 3 and 7 – 10.30.

Lymington Road, East End. Tel: 01590 626223

Dating back to 1825, the East End Arms is one of the few remaining traditional Forest pubs. It was bought a few years ago by a member of the pop group Dire Straits who decided to keep it that way. There is a public bar for the locals and a larger recently refurbished and extended comfortable lounge. A nice level circular walk, described in Mike Power's, 'Pub Walks in the New Forest' guides you across farm land and through attractive woodland with views across the Solent to the Isle of Wight.

Being a freehouse the choice of real ales is changed constantly but usually includes two regulars from the local Ringwood Brewery, Best Bitter and Fortyniner, also a guest like Summer Lightning from the Hop Back Brewery.

Food is served every lunch time except Monday and every evening between 7 and 9 but not Sunday. Expect to find on the menu delicious snacks like asparagus with a Stilton sauce, baguettes and ciabatta. Also dishes like loin of pork, a beef platter, lemon sole, rib eye steaks, thick cod fillet in tomato and basil sauce with salami and a pigeon breast with wine.

Dogs are welcome, and children away from the bar.

Opening times 11. 30 – 3 and 6 – 11, Sunday 12 – 10.30.

Hightown, Ringwood. Tel: 01425 472516

Several refurbishments over the years have not altered the character of this lovely old thatched pub. Originally two small 16th century cottages it was converted into a pub with two bars in the 1970's. Today there are three principal areas, the large comfortably furnished main bar, a smaller part panelled bar dominated by a large ingleook fireplace with a warm wood burning stove on a raised hearth and a small side room. Above the bare boarded and carpeted floor exposed brick walls support the partly beamed ceiling. Adjoining the pub is a converted barn catering for skittle parties, private functions and conferences. Al fresco drinkers and diners can sit on the sunny front lawns.

The pub was once part of Whitbread which was sold in 2001. On offer is a varied selection of real ales like Ringwood Best, Flowers Original, Wadworth 6X and Fullers London Pride. Also Whitbread Best, Heineken Best, Export, Stella and Strongbow cider.

Food is available every day 12 – 2.30 and 6 – 9. The printed menu presently lists seven starters followed by gammon steak, ham and eggs, sausage and mash, chicken tikka masala, chilli and lasagne. Fish dishes include a bake made with chunks of white fish and prawns in a creamy vegetable sauce topped with sliced potato. There are traditional pies of minted lamb, steak and kidney and steak and ale. Alternatively you might choose a speciality rack of ribs or just a snack which include jacket potatoes, baguettes and ploughman's.

Children welcome, dogs in pub only not restaurant area.

Opening times 11 – 11, Sunday 12 – 10.30.

Godshill, Fordingbridge. Tel: 01425 652462

Overlooking open Forest in a lovely sunny spot, the Fighting Cocks was built in 1927 and recently underwent complete refurbishment with the creation of an attractive family room with high chairs. The Foresters Bar has a padded window bench and a small seating area with a mix of tables and chairs and heated in winter by a warm wood burning stove. The dining room has a bare wood floor, a large brick fireplace with an open log fire and comfortable padded light wood chairs. Quieter in winter the pub positively buzzes with tourists in the season.

The well stocked bar in this managed house includes Ringwood Best and Wadworth 6X plus other guest ales. Also Stella, Guinness, Heineken Export, Strongbow and country wines. There is an 11-bin wine list.

Food times are 12 – 2 and 6 – 9 weekdays, Sunday 12 – 2.30 and 6 – 8.30. Blackboard specials might include venison and wild mushroom casserole, roast pheasant with red wine sauce, roast lamb shank, Cumberland sausage and red snapper with pesto. The printed menu lists several lunch time snacks such as fresh mussels – Thai style or with garlic butter, half a pint of prawns and basket meals. Also listed are baguettes, jacket potatoes and the 'Cocks' ploughman's. Main meals include homemade Agister's pie, sizzling strips of beef, liver and bacon, ratatouille, lasagne and ham, 'egggggs' and chips – sliced ham and as many eggs as you can eat. Traditional English puds include spotted dick, treacle tart and fruit crumble

Children welcome, dogs only in pub.

Weekday opening times all day 11 – 11, Sunday 12 – 10.30.

Four en-suite double rooms, one family.

Lymington Road, Setley. Tel: 01950 623447. e-mail: http://www.fillyinn.co.uk

This lovely wayside inn is reputed to be haunted. According to Roger Long in his book 'Haunted Inns of Hampshire' he tells the story of an un-named wealthy traveller going between Brockenhurst and Lymington who was robbed and murdered by three sailors and his body thrown into the river. Later they were in the Filly boasting about their exploits when they were overheard by the landlord who reported them to the authorities. They were subsequently arrested, hanged and their bodies left to rot near the Filly inn as a warning to others. For years afterwards their spirits were said to roam the inn looking for the landlord.

The Filly has two warm and welcoming bars heavily beamed with bare brick walls. The rear bar has a large open fireplace adorned with old animal traps. Furnishings are an assortment of farmhouse, tables, chairs and pews. Outside there is a large rear gravelled area with picnic benches

The well stocked bar of this freehouse has a good range of red and white wines plus two real ales, Ringwood Old Thumper and Ringwood Fortyniner.

As all food is freshly prepared to order it is advisable to ask the waiting time before ordering. Available 10 - 2.15 and 6.30 - 9. (9.30 weekends), the choice is between snacks like sandwiches, baguettes, assorted ploughman's and jacket potatoes or the popular carvery. Dishes from the blackboard might include Stilton and bacon burger or a curry. Also popular are homemade lasagne, homemade pie of the day, mushroom stroganoff, breaded seafood platter and home-cooked ham and eggs followed by syrup sponge with custard, toffee lemon meringue and syrup sponge with custard. There is a separate children's menu and for early birds a big breakfast served between 10 and 12 noon.

Children welcome.

Opening times 10 - 3 and 6 - 11, normal Sunday hours.

B & B accommodation, 3 stars with the English Tourist Board.

Monday night is quiz night

The Bridges, Ringwood. Tel: 01425 473185.

Squeezed between the Ringwood by-pass and the River Avon and accessed either direct from the main A31 or through Ringwood via West Street is the delightful Fish Inn an attractive 300 year old thatched pub. Recently re-thatched and refurbished, it has maintained much of its original charm and character. It is everything a good pub should be, good food and well-kept ale served in comfortable surroundings. There are two main seating areas heated by a warm wood burning stove and a third more intimate room having bare brick and timber plastered walls with a high pitched timbered roof sharing a second fireplace. In keeping with its name stuffed fish and associated regalia adorn the walls together with many other interesting artefacts. There are picnic benches in the garden running down to the edge of the river. Large no-smoking area.

For the discerning drinker four real ales are offered which includes Ringwood Fortyniner, Flowers Original, Strong's Best Bitter plus a guest along with Heineken Export and Stella Artois, Boddingtons and Whitbread Best Bitter, Murphys and Strongbow cider. There is a good selection of wines and fresh 'bean to cup' espresso, cappuccino or regular coffee.

The Fish majors on its food with a variety of choices – traditional and modern, continental and very English at affordable prices. Available all day 12 – 9.30 (Saturday 10 p.m. and Sunday 9 p.m.). The menu, chalked daily on the blackboard, takes advantage of seasonal changes, ensuring variety. Local produce is used where possible and all prepared and cooked on the premises. Lunchtime and evenings there is a choice of starters plus meals like minted lamb pie, Louisiana pork steak, bacon wrapped chicken with garlic and mushrooms and swordfish and shrimp salsa. A printed menu operates all day and there is a separate children's menu.

Children welcome, but dogs in garden only.

The Fish is open all day 11 – 11, Sunday 12 – 10.30.

Sunday night is quiz night in the winter.

Winkton, nr. Christchurch Tel: 01202 477283

Dating back to 1673, the Fisherman's Haunt is a very popular venue with locals and tourists alike. Refurbished since the last edition of this guide the well appointed and large comfortable interior is a series of linked rooms furnished to a very high standard. There is also a dining room and conservatory plus outside seating.

The pub is a freehouse with a well stocked bar which presently includes Bass, Ringwood Fortyniner, Gales HSB and GB.

A good menu is served 12 – 2 and 6.30 – 9. Apart from sandwiches and toasties, listed on the blackboard there are Fisherman's favourites like steak and kidney pie, ham, egg and chips, lasagne and curry of the day also a vegetarian choice such as Stilton and vegetable crumble plus a separate children's menu. Starters range from egg and prawns mayonnaise and Dorset pate to deep fried white bait and tomato and mushroom soup. Supplementing the menu are various steaks, chef's mixed grill, Cajun style chicken, pork loin steak. Separate menu for Saturday and Sunday evening has additions like tempting chicken Isabella – poached chicken filled with ham and asparagus, topped with a mornay sauce and finished under the grill.

Families are welcome, so too are dogs.

Opening times weekdays 10.30 – 2.30 and 5 – 11, Saturday all day 10.30 – 11 and Sunday all day 12 – 10.30.

18 rooms.

All Saint's Lane, Lymington. Tel: 01590 678931.

The Fisherman's Rest, an old smugglers haunt, can be reached from Belmore Lane, a turning at the top of the High Street. It is a lovely leafy area of Lymington surrounded by open fields. The interior is beautifully kept having low, light wood beams throughout and solid tables and farmhouse chairs on the part flag-stoned and part carpeted floor. The bar is in the centre serving all areas including the very attractive dining room. White plastic and blue painted furniture is positioned on the front patio making the most of the sunny position.

The pub is a freehouse offering imbibers a good selection of wines plus a couple of real ales from the Ringwood Brewery presently Best Bitter and Fortyniner.

Food times are 12 – 2.15 and 6.30 – 9.30, no food Sunday evening. The lunchtime bar menu lists imaginative starters like goats cheese tart with a green leaf salad, Caesar salad with smoked chicken, pan fried Hallounni cheese with an olive, tomato and seasonal leaf salad and creamy clam chowder with crispy croutons. Heading the main meals are fresh haddock in beer batter, smoked haddock, poached egg and hollandaise sauce on a toasted muffin, Thai green curry with tiger prawns served with sticky coconut rice and stir fry bean sprouts, spring onion and vegetables served with egg noodles in an oriental sauce. Additional meals on the more comprehensive evening menu include shredded duck breast on a rocket and orange salad and a filo basket with a wild mushroom and cream sauce followed by fillet of sea bass with a chilli and ginger salsa, pan fried king scallops with garlic and lemon and lamb shank served on mashed potato with a red wine and red currant sauce. Booking is advisable.

Dogs and families welcome.

Present opening hours all day every day 11 - 11, Sunday 12 – 10.30.

Station Road, Sway. Tel: 01590 682287.

Conveniently located on the southern edge of the New Forest between Brockenhurst, Lymington and New Milton this once Victorian coaching inn is today a friendly village local.

The 'village' bar at the front has traditional pub games whilst the comfortable lounge has an attractive wooden fireplace housing a warm log fire on cold winter evenings. Go through to the back and you enter the very attractive conservatory overlooking the large rear garden and children's play area. In the garden is a boules court which according the hosts is the biggest outside France.

Ringwood Best Bitter is the regular ale in this freehouse with a regular changing guest ale like Strongs Bitter.

The varied menu includes traditional English fayre, a hearty full English breakfast and daily blackboard specials. You might expect to see soup of the hour with a crusty baguette, homemade chicken liver pate and prawns piri piri. To follow there could be char-grilled barbary duck breast served on a bed of crispy leeks with gooseberry sauce, pink roasted rack of lamb, stuffed breast of chicken with mozzarella, spinach and smoked bacon served with a cream and garlic rocket sauce, chef's homemade moussaka and a meat or vegetarian lasagne. Sweet lovers can choose between bread and butter pudding or a crumble and custard.

Families welcome .

Weekday opening times are from 11 – 11 Sunday 12 – 10.30

Overnight accommodation is available, all rooms en-suite, with tea and coffee making facilities and colour television.

Lyndhurst Road, Ashurst. Tel: 02380 292331 Fax: 02380 292574
e-mail: forestinn.ashurst@whitbread.com

A warm welcome awaits you from the open fire in the main bar of this well run pub. To quote the landlord of this Whitbread tenanted pub, Alex Noble "A traditional inn serving traditional fayre to customers with traditional values"

Real ales on offer include Gales HSB and two from the local Ringwood Brewery, Best Bitter and True Glory. Also available Heineken, Stella Export and Strongbow cider plus a good selection of wines.

Food times in the week 12 – 2.30 and 6 – 8.45 Saturday and Sunday all day 12 – 8.45. Daily specials such as curry, chilli and tuna steaks supplement the main menu which lists a good choice of starters followed by dishes such as lamb shank – a tender mini leg smothered with gravy, traditional sausage and mash and steak and kidney pudding. There are several vegetarian dishes and a good selection of sweets.

Dogs welcome in the garden only, children welcome in pub.

Opening times all day every day 11 – 11, Sunday 12 – 10.30.

268 Woodlands Road, Woodlands, nr. Ashurst. Tel: 02380 293093.

Located in a quiet village lane, The Gamekeeper, built around 1880, was previously known as The Royal Oak when it was owned by Strong & Co of Romsey. Recently refurbished the large main beamed bar has quarry tiles beside the bar, country style furnishings on a carpeted floor and heated by a large warm wood burning stove. A back door leads to a conservatory beyond which is a paved patio area with large solid circular picnic benches. The cosy dining room has part panelled walls and dark wood furnishings also a small partly raised secure area with high chairs for family dining.

The pub is owned by Wadworth & Co, the Wiltshire based brewers, with a range of their real ales which include 6X and Henry's Original IPA.

Food is available 12 – 2.30 and 6.30 – 9.30, Sunday 12 - 3.30ish, no food in the evening. A printed menu is supplemented by a range of daily blackboard specials such as shepherds pie, beef curry and sausage and mash. Freshly made sandwiches, baguettes and jacket potatoes come with a good range of fillings as do the ploughman's. An all-day breakfast includes bacon, sausage, mushrooms, tomato, baked beans, hash browns, and black pudding. There is a selection of starters, fish, grills and roast chicken plus vegetarian meals and a children's menu.

Children and dogs welcome.

The pub open is all day 11 – 11, Sunday 12 – 10.30.

Bridge Street, Fordingbridge. Tel: 01425 652040. Fax: 652152

The George occupies a stunning position beside the fast flowing River Avon. During the winter of 2001 water entered the bar causing complete refurbishment but happily all was soon put right. The one main bar is on two levels, carpeted, warmly decorated and heated by an open log fire. A conservatory on the back goes right to the water's edge and there are tables on the patio at the side. Entrance to the car park is just north of the bridge under the archway.

The George is a Wayside Inn, part of the Unique Collection, very well run by the new licensees Steve and Pauline Tester. Beers on offer include Fullers London Pride, Wadworth 6X, Ringwood Best and Ringwood Fortyniner together with Heineken, Stella, Guinness and Strongbow cider.

Food is available every day all day between 12 and 9. Apart from four daily specials such as homemade pies, Moroccan kebabs and lamb rogan josh the menu lists roasted pepper and mushroom bruschetta, deep fried Brie, field mushrooms stuffed with bacon and cheese and potted game pie. Wild Alaskan salmon is served with lemon pepper butter whilst salmon and thyme fishcakes come with mixed salad and a sour cream and cucumber relish. For vegetarians there is Mediterranean cous cous and pasta with a creamy spinach and basil sauce whilst steak eaters have a choice of Aberdeen Angus rib eye or rump. Also listed are steak and ale pie, marinated shoulder of lamb, a thick cut gammon steak and smothered chicken.

Children welcome in the conservatory or lounge, dogs in the bar.

Opening times all day 11 – 11, Sunday 12 – 10.30.

Brook, Cadnam. Tel: 02380 813359.

Brook is signed from junction 1 of the M27. This very attractive two-storey white painted thatched inn dates from the early 19th century but the building is some 400 years old beginning life as a wheelwrights and coffin-makers. Recent refurbishment has in no way spoilt what is essentially a very good local. Two cosy low beamed rooms to the left and right are heated by wood burning stoves in raised hearths with an assortment of solid tables, chairs and benches. Both bars display unique leather sheets branded with the marks of the commoners whose animals have the right to graze the Forest. There is a small side room with a pool table in winter but used as a children's room in summer. At the rear is an attractive, comfortable restaurant beyond which is a patio and lawned garden.

The inn is a pub partnership with a good choice of real ales which presently include three winter ales Gales HSB, Wadworth 6X and Ringwood Best with Strongs being added for the summer.

Good food is served every day from 12 – 2.30 & 6.30 - 9 . Always available are sandwiches, French bread sticks, 'Dragon' platters and jacket potatoes. From the set menu starters listed include homemade soup, calamari strips with seafood dip and Monterey melters filled with cream cheese and served with a garlic dip. There is a good choice of salads, fish dishes and old favourites like ham and eggs and homemade steak and kidney pie. Lunch time specials are listed on the blackboard with more choice in the evening such as smoked salmon strips in a honey and mustard sauce, steak and kidney pie and faggots with garden peas.

Families welcome, dogs in the bar only.

Opening times 11 – 3 & 6 – 11.30, Sunday 12 – 3 & 7 – 10.30.

Keyhaven, nr. Lymington. Tel: 01590 642391

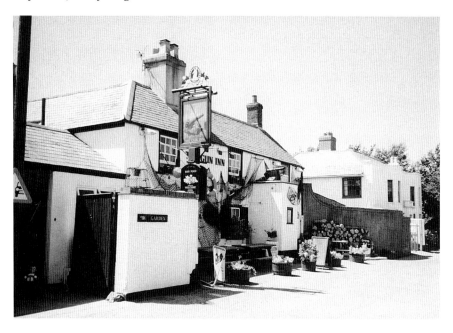

Named after Col. Hawker whose hunting gun claimed numerous victims and resided next door in 'Hawkers Cottage', this 17th century white painted inn occupies an enviable spot close to the harbour at Keyhaven and its popular sailing club. In its time it has also been a chapel and a mortuary. Fishnets adorn the outside walls whilst guns are displayed inside on the large brick fireplace which houses a warm winter fire. Furnishings consist of farmhouse tables and chairs and comfortable red pew seating whilst the walls are adorned with nautical regalia and brightly shining copper and brass items.

The well stocked bar of this Whitbread partnership offers a very good choice of drinks which includes 150 malt whiskies and six real ales. Presently available are Ringwood Fortyniner, Flowers Original, Boddingtons Bitter, Marston's Pedigree, Morland Old Speckled Hen and Brakspear Bitter.

Popular with diners, good food is served daily from 12 – 2.30 and 6 – 9.30. Apart from snacks like ploughman's, jacket potatoes, soup and sandwiches a full menu is available offering dishes such as supreme of salmon with crab and lobster in season. For the sweet toothed there is a good range of traditional puddings. A playing card system marks your turn.

Children are welcome and dogs too, <u>strictly on leads and under control.</u>

Opening hours 11 – 3 and 6 – 11 with usual Sunday opening.

Car parking is at the 'pay and display' across the road which operates from March to October but in the wintertime is free.

Linwood. Tel: 01425 473973. Web site: www.highcornerinn. com

Built originally as a farmhouse in the 17th century, the very popular High Corner Inn is remotely situated in the heart of the Forest down a long gravel track. Several cosy rooms radiate from the main dark wood bar heated by an open log fire in winter. There is another bar at the bottom of a flight of steps, a restaurant and function room. Outside there is a terrace and large lawn with picnic benches.

The inn recently changed hands and is now owned by Wadworth and Co Ltd. Real ales include 6X, Henry's IPA and Adnams Bitter.

Food is served 12 - 2 and 6.30 - 9.30 (Sunday 9) The set menu includes home-made soup, deep fried breaded goats cheese, avocado fan filled with salmon and pan fried mushrooms in red wine and tomato sauce. Main meals might include homemade beef chilli, smoked bacon lasagne, deep fried cod fillet in homemade batter and mini breaded lobster thermidor. Prime Scottish steaks, sirloin and rump are also listed as is an 8 oz lamb steak marinated in apricot and rosemary, a brace of locally made turkey, bacon and leek sausages plus 'lite bites' and sand-wiches, hot meat sandwiches and interesting ploughman's. Poachers has a slice of home-cooked honey roast ham and two sausages served with crusty bread, salad, chutney and a pickled onion. Daily specials might include tomato and basil soup, homemade steak and black pudding pie, leek macaroni and blue cheese bake, steamed salmon steak with lemon and fresh herbs and homemade vegetable quiche. Children's activity menu at the food bar.

Children under 14 are not allowed in the bar only in the family rooms.

Opening times Monday to Friday 11 - 3 and 6 – 11, Saturday 11 – 11, Sunday 12 – 10.30.

Southampton Road, Battramsley, nr. Lymington. Tel: 01590 23291

It is said that a pub is as good as its landlord, this is never more true than at the lovely Hobler. Pip Stevens, the longstanding landlord has built a reputation for excellent food and well conditioned real ales served in a traditional pub atmosphere. It is not a smart pub but it is a great pub warm and welcoming. The building is over 400 years old and was once a combined butcher's, bakers and pub. It is named after a hobler – a man who would hoble horses by tying their front legs together so they could feed but not run off. Accommodation is in two separate areas with mats on the bare wood floors, a mix of furnishings and lots of interesting regalia displayed all around. On a cold days warm log fires burn in the open grates.

The well-stocked bar includes a good choice of real ales and wines.

Not suprisingly the inn has won several awards for its excellent food which is available daily 12 – 2 and 6 – 10. From simple snacks such as soup, ploughman's and chicken liver pate the menu extends to dishes like smoked venison – thinly sliced filet with a mixed salad of grapes, walnut and cherry tomatoes finished with parmesan shavings, mint and lime dressing. Main dishes range from salmon royale – supreme oven baked served on stir fried vegetables with prawns and smoked salmon finished with a herb mayonnaise and chicken goujons seasoned with five spices, crispy fried on a bed of tomato concasse with melted mozarella cheese and leaves to tasty salads which include one with duck breast another having avocado and crispy bacon and one with smoked chicken, salmon and prawns.

Excellent spacious garden with children's play area.

Opening times 11 – 2.30 and 6 – 11 Sunday 12 – 10.30.

Woodgreen, nr. Fordingbridge. Tel : 01725 510739

Woodgreen is indeed fortunate to have such a splendid pub within its midst, voted by many to be one of the best in the Forest, it was originally stables built over one hundred years ago. Heated by an open fire, the small cosy front bar has various bird prints and photographs on the walls, to the left is a locals bar and to the right two dining areas, one added fairly recently, which can seat up to fifty. There is a sunny rear garden with picnic benches plus more benches running along the entire front and side patio.

Once a freehouse, the pub is now owned by Hall & Woodhouse, very well run by the present licensees. The well stocked bar which has some good malt whiskies and Hofbrau Premium and Export lager also offers real ale drinkers a choice of three Ringwood Best, the lovely golden Tanglefoot and King & Barnes Sussex.

The pub has always been popular for its very good Sunday roast but a full menu is also available every day 12 – 2 and 7 – 9.30. In addition to daily specials like broccoli and Stilton soup, old English mushrooms in a cream and garlic sauce whilst a fanned avocado is set on a bed of salad and topped with prawns in a light Marie Rose sauce. Speciality sausages heads the main courses followed by chicken in Stilton and brandy, beef and ale pie and honey roast smoked ham. Fish dishes range from a whole dressed crab to fish 'n' chips. There are vegetarian dishes, salads and a children's menu plus ploughman's, jacket potatoes and fresh filled sandwiches for those just wanting a snack.

Families are welcome in the dining areas and dogs on a lead in the bar.

Opening times are from 11 – 3 and 6 –11, Sunday 12 – 3 and 7 – 10.30.

Ashlet Creek, nr. Fawley. Tel: 02380 891305.

Take the Fawley road and half a mile from the village follow the brown signs for Ashlet Creek and you will find the Jolly Sailor. Painted blue and white, the pub occupies an enviable position overlooking the creek, fields and water beyond. Dark wooden panels are much in evidence in the main bar which has tables, chairs and benches. A central fireplace and open fire serves the bar on the other side where typical pub games such as pool, darts, dominoes and cribbage are played. Bench seating is positioned all the way along the front wall maximising the sunny aspect and unspoilt view.

The well stocked bar in this Whitbread partnership includes Ringwood Best, Marston's Pedigree and Boddingtons Bitter plus Guinness, several lagers and ciders.

Food is excellent and includes a large Spanish menu with tapa-sized portions. A 'Jolly' breakfast is served between 12 and 3 but food times generally are 12 – 2.30 and 6 – 9 Saturday and Sunday all day 12 – 9. Snacks like baguettes and jacket potatoes are available from the menu also starters range from crispy mushrooms to wings of fire and main meals from butterfly Cajun chicken breast to steaks served sizzling on a skillet with tomato, mushrooms and onion rings. Available as a starter or a tapa, the Spanish menu includes ensaladilla de patata – salad of potato, orange, French beans, tuna, egg and olives and berengena frita – deep fried aubergine sticks with honey dip. Main courses which are also available as tapas include estofado de terncra – a stew of beef with carrots, mushrooms, peas and white wine sauce, albondigas – seasoned meat balls served with two sauces and tortas Espanolas – griddle cakes made with either prawns or cauliflower. Blackboard specials include 5 or 6 types of authentic Indian curries and vegetarian dishes.

Dogs and children both equally welcome.

Opening times all day 11 –11, Sunday 12 – 10.30.

Eling Hill, Eling. Tel: 02380 868899.

The King Rufus, a two-storey cream and green painted inn, is one of two pubs that face each other at a small road junction, both busy, both different in character. This beautifully kept Victorian inn simply oozes with character. Inside there are three open plan rooms and a rear restaurant. The right-hand room has a bare stone floor, warm wood burning stove with masses of brightly shining copper and brassware and a pine dresser in the corner brimming full with china and artefacts. Old photographs hang on the walls in the area opposite which are painted in a very attractive green contrasting perfectly with the Victorian fireplace.

Owned by Enterprise Inns the regular ales are Ringwood Best, Gales HSB plus a couple of changing guests.

Food is available 12 – 2 and 6.30 – 9.30, Sunday 7. The snack menu lists baguettes, doorstep sandwiches, jacket potatoes and ploughman's, plus cauliflower cheese, homemade beef burger, omelette and the Rufus brunch – sausage, eggs, bacon, fried bread, black pudding, mushrooms, beans and tomatoes. A set two-course menu is available daily with dishes such as gammon egg and chips, chicken Kiev, homemade steak and ale pie, sausage and mash with onion gravy and chilli. Additionally there are blackboard specials like breaded mushrooms stuffed with crab meat and king prawns with a garlic cream sauce followed by breaded lemon sole, pork tenderloin in Calvados and cream sauce, whilst vegetarians could opt for spicy pasta or a nut roast with chips.

Dogs and children welcome.

Opening times 11.30 – 2.30 and 6 – 11. Normal Sunday hours.

Forest Edge Road, Nomansland, Wilts. Tel/Fax: 01794 390246
e-mail: thelambinn@amservenett

Idyllically situated in an enviable position the Lamb Inn lies right on the Hampshire/Wiltshire border so that one can sit in the Wiltshire Bar and watch cricket played in Hampshire on the green opposite. Many years ago both counties had different closing times so customers simply moved from one bar to the other. Comfortably furnished they have white painted and black wood walls adorned with various Forest memorabilia like antlers and a fox head. The bar itself has an interesting thatched canopy. There is a children's play area, seating on the sunny front terrace and a private garden with lights in the evening. Live music every Saturday evening.

A leased house, the bar presently offers real ale drinkers a choice of five, Ringwood Best, Whitbread Best, Wadworth 6X, London Pride and Strongs. Also Guinness, Heineken, Export and Thatcher's cider.

Generously portioned bar food is available every day 12 – 2.30 and 6.30 – 9.30 (9 on Sunday). There are the usual snacks such as sandwiches, ploughman's, filled jacket potatoes and old favourites like steak and ale pie. There is usually a curry of the day, mixed grill, lasagne and vegetarians dishes. Daily special on offer might include fillet steak Rossini, chicken and ham pie, skate wing in black butter and ricotta cheese cannelloni.

Dogs are welcome inside, children too but only if dining.

Opening times Monday – Thursday 11 – 3 and 6 – 11, Friday and Saturday all day 11 – 11, Sunday 12 – 10.30.

Burley Road, Winkton. Tel: 01425 672427

Located just over the border in Dorset, the Lamb Inn is nevertheless on the fringe of the New Forest and well worth including in this guide. It is still a traditional pub having a public bar heated by an open log fire with traditional pub games such as darts and shove halfpenny. There is a comfortable lounge, a separate à la carte restaurant and outside patio and lawned beer garden with good children's play area.

The Lamb is a freehouse and thus able to offer a constantly changing range of real ales together with the regular Ringwood Bitter.

Food is served lunchtime and in the evening. The menu chalked on the blackboard lists the usual ploughman's, sandwiches plus homemade steak and ale pie and venison sausages etc. Daily specials might include poached salmon hollandaise, a luxury chicken Kiev, half a shoulder of lamb in red wine, fillet of beef stroganoff and roast duck à la orange. Tempting sweets such as ginger sponge with a lemon sauce, spotty dick, jam sponge and treacle tart will be sure to tempt you. There is a separate children's menu plus a vegetarians board listing meals like vegetable pasta and lasagne.

Families welcome, dogs allowed in public bar.

Opening times 11 – 3 and 5.30 – 11, Saturday 11 – 11, normal Sunday hours except July and August when the pub is open all day.

Jazz band on Wednesday which is also curry night.

Bucklers Hard, Beaulieu. Tel/Fax: 01590 616253

Located within the Master Builders House Hotel, the Yachtsman's Bar is situated at the river end of Bucklers Hard, one of the most picturesque villages in Hampshire, famous for shipbuilding since 1698, the Maritime Museum records the history where Nelson's fleet was built from New Forest Oak. It is said a smuggler's tunnel leads from the comfortably furnished bar with a stone floor, open log fireplace, original beams and adorned with various shipping photographs.

A freehouse, the bar has a wide range of drinks which include Burton Ale, Tetley's Cask and Smooth, Carlsberg Export, Guinness, Strongbow cider and various malts. Clotted cream teas served between 3 and 5.

Food is available every day 12 – 2ish and 6.30 – 9. The menu, supplemented by specials such as spicy pork with rice, presently lists snacks like soup and ploughman's followed by avocado, bacon and poached egg salad, organic sausages served with mash and gravy, fish pie, dressed crab, a prawn salad and minute steak with crushed potato, mushrooms and tomatoes. Lunchtime additions - toasted ciabattas. Separate children's menu.

Children and dogs both equally welcome.

Opening times all day 11 – 11, Sunday 12 – 10.30.

Accommodation available in hotel.

Kings Saltern Road, Lymington. Tel : 01590 672160

From the marina car park you can enter directly into the garden and walk across the lawn to the rear of the Mayflower Inn which is situated in an enviable position overlooking the river. The plush, part wood panelled main bar which has a regal blue carpet, curtains and matching blue upholstered furniture leads to a partitioned area for more intimate drinking and dining. Beside the bar is a bare boarded area where a grand looking carved wooden chair is positioned. Beyond the bar is another comfortable seating area with a red carpeted floor and a brick fireplace in the end wall housing a warm log fire. The large rear lawn has picnic benches and a children's play area in one corner.

The inn is a Whitbread partnership offering a good choice of drinks which include three real ales, London Pride, Ringwood Best and Flowers Original; plus Heineken, Stella and Strongbow cider.

The light lunchtime menu includes dishes like Caesar salad and baked goat's cheese en croute with a cranberry dressing plus a range of snacks such as toasted filled breads, ploughman's and baguettes. Specials chalked daily on the blackboard might include liver and bacon with mash and onion gravy, fillet steak and whole grain mustard mash, smoked haddock with spring onion mash, grilled lamb steak, leek Roquefort tart salad, grilled lemon sole and cheese, tomato and basil ravioli.

Opening times all day 11 – 11, Sunday 12 – 10.

Six en-suite bedrooms.

Avon, nr. Christchurch. Tel: 01425 672432.

Built around the time of Queen Victoria's birth (1819), this very attractive pub was aptly named. The Victorian style interior, recently refurbished is spacious but comfortable with cosy intimate areas for quiet drinking or dining. Outside there is an attractive canopied patio and large beer garden with a good children's play area safely stretching right down to the river.

Part of the Hall & Woodhouse managed estate, the bar includes two of their favourite real ales, Badger Best and the delightful golden Tanglefoot also Ringwood Best, plus Guinness, Hofbrau Premium and Export lager.

Food is served daily 12 – 2 and 6.30 – 9.30, Sunday 12 – 3 and 6.30 – 9.30. Typically there could be Hong King chicken and favourites like steak kidney and Tanglefoot pie. In addition you might prefer to choose something from the black-board such as Mozzarella and tomato salad, pan fried garlic mushrooms, pork smokey – diced pork and bacon in a cream sauce, lamb and apricot pie, chicken breast stuffed with olives and Brie and grilled black bream with clams and mussels. Vegetarians meals range from sweet vegetable masala and spicy bean wrap to a wild mushroom tagliatelle and Brie salad. A two-course lunch special is available in the week; also catered for are those with small appetites.

Children and dogs welcome.

Weekday opening time 11.30 – 2.30, Sunday 12 – 3 and 6 – 10.30.

Pinkney Lane, Bank, Lyndhurst. Tel: 02380 282350.

Originally the Royal Oak, this lovely atmospheric inn dates from 1719 when it is said a tunnel linked nearby Queens House in Lyndhurst enabling the Royals to escape in the event of trouble. Often missed by motorists, the inn is located in a lovely area of forest just a short distance from the busy A35. Cattle and horses regularly stand in the shade of the front porch which leads directly into the low beamed and boarded open plan bar. Rustic furniture, neatly positioned on the bare boarded floor consists of scrubbed pine tables, a mix of chairs and unusual adapted milk churn bar stools. A log fire is housed in an attractive wood and tiled fireplace. Additional seating can be found in the small rear garden and a covered area at the front.

The inn is a freehouse offering a choice of drinks and country wines, also four real ales like Bass and Ringwood Best plus winter ales such as Black Country Special Bitter from the Dudley Brewery and Ringwood Brewery's Porter.

Food times Monday to Thursday 12 – 2 and 6.30 – 9, weekends 12 – 2 & 6.30 – 9.30 Sunday 12 – 2.30 & 7 – 9. The menu chalked daily on the blackboard includes snacks like marmalade and Stilton 'Oak' doorsteps, garlic chicken goujons, beef bourgignon, homemade steak and kidney pie, chicken Kiev, lamb curry, fillet of plaice, jumbo battered cod, bowl of hot chilli and a cheesy country bake served with salad and French fries. Bread and butter pudding heads the sweet list followed by sticky toffee pudding, crazy about coconut- coconut mousse on a biscuit base served with chocolate sauce and toffee apple and pecan pie.

Well behaved children welcome, also clean dogs.

Opening times 11. 30 – 2.30 and 6 – 11, Saturday 11.30 – 3, Sunday 12 – 3 and 7 – 10.30.

Hythe Road, Marchwood. Tel: 02380 867752

Amiable proprietor, Ron Longman, converted these 200-year-old cottages into the delightful Pilgrim Inn enhanced further by the beautiful award-winning gardens. Under a thatched roof this well kept country inn positively bursts with character. The large L-shaped bar has solid oak beams, a real log fire and lots of interesting regalia. Comfortable velvet seating around the walls provides cosy corners for quiet conversation without the intrusions of fruit or vending machines.

The Pilgrim is a freehouse with a good selection of drinks. Real ales include Draught Bass, and Directors plus Worthington Best, John Smiths, mild and Guinness, Kronenberg, Fosters, Carling Black Label, Old Rascal and Stowford Press cider on draught. Also available are Gales Country wines and an excellent French house wine

The typical pub menu is one of the best for value in the area and includes snacks such as sandwiches and homemade soup plus a daily specials board listing home-made specialities like liver and bacon casserole, avocado and prawn salad, gammon hock, hot steak sandwich, dressed crab salad, chilli, chicken curry and cottage pie. There are a choice of four roasts, vegetarian dishes and tempting desserts.

Opposite the inn is the Pilgrim's Progress, a beautifully appointed restaurant with tasteful décor offering both à la carte and table d'hôte menus of outstanding quality including vegetarian dishes. It is ideally suited for both intimate dining or special occasions. There is a small private dining room and the restaurant is also available for functions.

Opening times Monday – Friday 11 – 2.30, Saturday 11 – 3 and 6 – 11, Sunday all day 12 – 10.30. Pilgrim's Progress Friday and Saturday evenings.

Sway Road, Tiptoe. Tel: 01425 610185.

Originally a farm, the Plough Inn dates from 1630, evidence of which can be seen on a small section of wall behind a glass screen. In recent years the pub has been comfortably refurbished and extended. Low wooden ceilings and a large open fireplace are features of the main L-shaped bar, whilst a small cosy side room is dominated by a large wooden dining table. At the back is a very attractive dining room with an interesting fireplace and old farm implements hanging from the high pitched wooden ceiling. A ghost called Jack is reputed to haunt the inn but generally only appears when there are changes at the inn. There are picnic benches at the front and in the rear beer garden.

The inn is a Whitbread partnership presently serving just the one real ale Ringwood Best.

Food is available lunch times in winter, Monday to Wednesday 12 – 2, Thursday to Sunday 12 – 2.30. Evenings, Monday – Wednesday 6.30 – 8.30 (9 on the other days). Summertime i.e. school holidays, all day 12 – 9. Changed daily the choice listed on the blackboard includes a range of meals to suit all appetites.

Children are welcome but only in the dining room, whilst well-controlled dogs are permitted in the bar and garden.

Opening times all day 12 – 11, Sunday 10.30.

The Cross, Burley. Tel: 01425 403423

Popular with visitors, picturesque Burley is one of few Forest villages open to animals. Ponies, donkeys and cattle roam free and often congregate outside the many small gift shops and village pubs. The Queens Head has been satisfying local thirsts since 1630 but refurbished over the years. The last major renovation sadly saw the demise of the original sunken Festival Bar – early photographs on the wall now the only record. Today the interior is mostly open plan but comfortably furnished with many cosy seating areas heated by winter log fires. The pub is steeped in history much of it linked to smuggling indeed a smuggler's horse is reputed to be buried near the bar and pistols, coins and guns have been unearthed over the years. There is a large garden and seats at the front.

Originally part of Whitbread, the inn has a well stocked bar with several real ales including the local Ringwood Best and Fortyniner.

Hearty food is served all day every day and includes the usual pub fayre such as warming soups, ploughman's, jacket potatoes, steak and kidney pie and homemade country dishes.

Dogs and families welcome away from the bar

Opening times 10.30 – 11, Sunday 12 – 10.30

Boldre, nr. Lymington. Tel: 01590 673177. Fax: 01590 67403

Peacefully located at Boldre, the inn is close to St John's Church and Spinners Garden, known for its rare shrubs. The very attractive exterior enhanced during summer with a lovely floral display is but a taste of what is about to greet you once inside. Four very atmospheric, connecting rooms, one non-smoking have assorted sturdy furnishings and heated by two open log fires. One of the smaller rooms still has in place the original black range surrounded by old cooking implements and copper kettles. Numerous brightly shining artefacts, farm tools, prints, mugs, plates and animal traps are displayed on the walls and from the heavily beamed ceilings.

New licensees are maintaining the traditions of this excellent Eldridge Pope pub. Royal Oak, Hardy Country Ale and Directors are dispensed by hand pump whilst those who prefer wine can choose from 44, a good number of them offered by the glass.

Popular with diners the menu is available every day 12 – 2.30 and 6.30 - 9.30. A choice of freshly made sandwiches and hearty ploughman's supplement the menu which typically starts with homemade smoked fish cakes, the chef's own pork and duck pate and salmon and prawn rillettes. Main courses include pan-fried calves liver and bacon, crispy duck in a basket, grilled Cumberland sausage and a lamb leg steak. Vegetarian and pasta dishes include broccoli and Stilton pasta shells, a vegetable casserole and red onion and apple tart. There are summer salads and tempting sweets like whisky bread and butter pudding.

No children under 14 or dogs allowed in the bar, but all welcome in the spacious grounds.

Inn open all day 11 – 11, usual Sunday hours.

Linwood. Tel: 01425 475792

Very popular with tourists and locals alike, this very atmospheric Forest inn has been quenching thirsts for as long as I can remember although it was originally the village post office. Attractively painted in red, the warm and welcoming open plan interior has a mix of solid wooden tables, chairs and bench seats on a plank floor. A log fire in the raised hearth is a welcome site on cold winter mornings. To the rear of the inn is a raised area, which is set aside for family dining. There are also seats at the front and on the heated side patio.

Owned by Wadworth, the pub is well managed by Paul Adams, an enterprising manager, who decided in April 1998 to brew real ale on the premises. The first brew was called Forest Gold and in October of the same year Tom's Tipple was introduced initially as a winter brew but now a permanency.

A very good menu is available every lunchtime 12 – 2 and in the evenings Monday to Thursday 6.30 – 9.30, Friday and Saturday 6.30 – 10 and Sunday 6.30 - 8.30. Supplemented by the daily specials board snacks include Forester's, trawler's and poacher's lunches plus light bites like sandwiches and jacket potatoes. There are starters such as homemade soup, deep fried spinach and feta goujons and the inn's own garlic bread topped with a choice of mushrooms, ham and pineapple or chilli finished with melted cheese. Main courses range from home-cooked sliced ham and speciality sausages to a home-made pie of the day and a vegetarian special. Children's activity menu available at the food bar.

Opening times all day 11 – 11 in summer, winter closed between 3 and 6.
Camp site at the rear.

Bashley Common Road, Wootton. Tel: 01425 610360

A stained glass door depicting the rising sun is but one of the original features of this rebuilt Victorian pub bedecked in summer with a colourful floral display and occupying an open sunny Forest position. Victorian décor pervades the large bar which is heated by an open log fire and extends into the original 'L'-shaped, bare-boarded public bar area, finished in green with similar painted farmhouse furniture and heated by a warm wood burning stove. Moving towards the rear is a partly enclosed heated patio with high chairs beyond which is an open patio and raised decking area with a good children's play area.

Ringwood Best is the regular real ale supported by a couple of guests like Hartleys XB and Adnams. Also Murphy's stout, Heineken and Stella.

Food is served all day 12 – 10. Blackboard specials supplement the menu which lists Cajun chicken, beef stroganoff, chicken tikka masala, lamb tagine, seared salmon with lemon and black pepper butter, chicken lasagne and a tuna and pasta bake. In addition to snacks like ploughman's and 'lite bites', traditional fayre includes lamb's liver and bacon casserole, steak and kidney pie and chicken, ham and leek pie. Vegetarian meals range from spinach, mushroom and tomato lasagne and harvest and leek crumble to cheesy vegetable bake and mushroom and red pepper stroganoff. Sunday roast and 'junior menu'.

Dogs and children welcome.

Pub open all day 11 – 11, usual Sunday hours.

Overnight accommodation.

Hill Top, Beaulieu. Tel/Fax: 01590 612228

Steeped in history, Beaulieu was once a finishing school for secret agents 1941 – 1945. Nearby Exbury gardens, the home of Lionel de Rothschild, covers 250 acres with rare trees and a huge collection of rhododendrons and azaleas, whilst the Montagu Motor Museum has one of the finest collection of vintage vehicles in the country.

Built in the early 1800's, the Royal Oak 'which stands at the crossroads of history' was originally two smallholdings. The first recorded licensee was John Ward in 1848 who was a saddle and harness maker. He was followed in 1852 by Benjamin Ward, a tailor. The inn, popular with locals and visitors alike, enjoys a splendid position with views across the heath.

Run by the same licensees since 1988, the bar has a good choice of real ales presently Ringwood Best, Flowers Original and Green King Old Speckled Hen and Abbot Ale.

Food times are 11.30 – 2.15 and 6 – 9, (Saturday 9.15), Sunday 12 – 2.30 and 6.45 – 9. The menu is listed daily on the blackboard with many home-made specials plus the usual snacks like sandwiches and ploughman's. Summer barbecues and private parties catered for.

Children welcome inside, but dogs only in the garden.

Weekday opening times 11 – 3 and 6 – 11, Sunday 12 – 10.30.

Downton, nr. Lymington Tel: 01590 642297

Dating back to 1695, the Royal Oak is a traditional pub having a series of inter-connected, low beamed rooms, each with its own open fireplace. Lots of brightly shining regalia adorn the walls and the furnishings are in a comfortable country style. There is an attractive rear garden.

The inn is now part of the Laural Pub Company, very well run by the new tenants Bob and Suzee Bevis who took over in December 2000. The well stocked bar includes three real ales Gales HSB and Ringwood Best plus a guest like Charles Wells Bombardier.

A very good and imaginative menu is available weekdays 12 – 2.30 (Sunday 3) and every evening. There are two blackboards, one lists only fresh fish dishes, heading the other are starters like homemade smoked mackerel pate, Thai fish-cakes and a starter for two to share – an oven baked Camembert studded with garlic and fresh herbs served with French bread and a red onion marmalade. Main courses range from supreme of chicken filled with mozzarella, oven roasted tomatoes and fresh basil with a fresh tomato and cream sauce and salmon, monkfish and scallop kebabs served on a bed of basmati rice with a creamy curry sauce to vegetarian pan fried button mushrooms crepes in a cream and garlic sauce covered in cheese to chef's steak special – fillet filled with scallops and prawns.

Dogs and children equally welcome.

Opening times 11.30 – 2.30 and 6 – 11, summer Saturday all day 11 – 11, Sunday 12 – 10.30.

Fritham. Tel: 02380 812606, Fax: 02380 814066.

Traditional Forest pubs are a rarity these days but seek out The Royal Oak at Fritham and you have found one of the best. Still part of a working farm, the pub was built sometime in the 17th century and has changed little in all that time. New owners have recently taken over and generally set about smartening the pub up, in my opinion for the better. Under a thatched roof, the small simply furnished front bar has bare wood flooring and heated by an open log fire. A doorway leads to a real snug which positively oozes with character enhanced by haphazardly leaning walls. Nicely furnished the small room has been lightened by the addition of discreet roof lights in the low closely boarded ceiling. The main feature of the room is the warm open log fire on a raised bed, which is set in a very large fireplace. Centrally heated toilets are across the yard, modern and immaculately kept. There is seating in the large garden outside.

The pub is a freehouse personally run by the new licensees Neil and Pauline McCulloch who intend to keep the pub just the way it is. Beer is excellent and still served traditionally straight from the barrel. CAMRA made it their pub of the year for South Hampshire in 1999 and 2000. The list includes Ringwood Best, True Glory and Fortyniner also Gales Country wines and an excellent wine list.

Food is only available at lunchtime between 12 and 2 (summer 2.30) and includes homemade winter soups, quiches and assorted ploughman's. There is the occasional pig roast and summer barbecue. Meals can be provided in the winter by prior arrangement.

Dogs and children both equally welcome.

Opening times Monday – Friday 11 - 3 and 6 - 11, Saturday all Day 11 - 11, Sunday 12 - 10.30.

68 High Street, Fordingbridge. Tel: 01425 651820. Fax: 651825.

Located in the centre of Fordingbridge, the Ship Inn is a Victorian coaching inn having just undergone a £250,000 refurbishment. The welcoming bar area has an open fire and wood panelled walls.

Five real ales are presently on offer in this Green King tenanted house which include their Abbot Ale, Triumph and IPA plus a couple of changing guest ales and 15 fine wines by the bottle or glass and to accompany them a bowl of marinated olives.

The regularly changing menu is to a high standard and available all week 12 – 2 and 6 – 9.30. Typically to start there are several wrapped tortillas, oven baked mushrooms with Stilton and red wine and a tower of avocado, prawns and mayonnaise. Traditionalists might like to follow with pan fried lamb's liver and bacon with mash and red wine gravy or local sausages served with mash and rich onion gravy.

Children and dogs both welcome. Play area in garden.

Weekday opening times 12 – 3 and 5.30 – 11, Saturday 12 – 3 and 6 – 11, Sunday 12 – 3 and 6 – 10.30.

Four bedrooms (one a family room) individually furnished to the highest standards with en-suite bathrooms, Sky TV and direct dial phone.

THE SHOE INN 72

Salisbury Road, Plaitford nr. Romsey. Tel/Fax: 01794 322397.
e-mail: aart@anoordijk.freeserve.co.uk

On a trip to the Forest a visit to The Shoe Inn is a must. Built in 1420, a beautifully crafted thatched roof protects the original inn, which took its name from the cavalry troops who frequented the inn when travelling from the garrison in Salisbury to the port of Marchwood. Seen from the main road, it's an attractive black and white half-timbered structure, built around 1640 when the inn became a posting station for mail coaches. A tollgate was constructed across the road and the landlord made responsible for collecting the King's tolls. The interior of the Shoe is as inviting as the outside having old world charm, real fires and many bygones on display.

The last New Forest highwayman, John Taylor was caught drinking here and subsequently hanged on nearby Plaitford Common. Queen Victoria once stopped here on route to the Isle of Wight. Along side the inn is what used to be the main road between Salisbury and Southampton.

The Shoe is a freehouse well run by the hosts Jeni and Aart Noordijk offering a good selection of lagers, draught beers, an extensive choice of wines and spirits plus three real ales which usually include Wadworth 6X and a Ringwood brew.

Food is available every lunchtime and evening. On offer is an appetising choice of homemade soups and starters, varied main dishes, daily specials like shank of lamb and T-bone steaks and some irresistible *'Go on indulge yourself'* homemade desserts. In good weather you can enjoy your meal in the attractive beer garden.

Well behaved dogs are welcome in the bar together with children.

The shoe opens from 11 – 3ish and 6 – 11, weekdays and 12 – 3ish and 6 – 10.30 on Sunday.

Entertainment includes pool, darts, dominoes, Irish & folk music on Friday evenings and blues and rock on Sunday evenings.

Swan Green, Lyndhurst. Tel: 02380 28203.
e-mail: swaninn.lyndhurst@whitbread.com

Attractively adorned with colourful flower tubs and hanging baskets, this two-storey 18th century inn occupies a spot just outside Lyndhurst opposite the picturesque village green. The main bar has a heavily, low-beamed ceiling, bare boarded floors and flagstones by the bar. Two comfortable armchairs are perfectly positioned to take advantage of the warm log fire in the corner. Away from the bar, cosy seating areas extend all the way round the side and through to the back where patrons sitting in a raised area have a lovely view over open countryside. A bar billiards table is positioned in an area at the side. The sign outside aptly sums up the pub: 'Relax with real fires, real food and real ales'

The Swan is a managed pub offering a selection of real ales, which presently include Ringwood Best, plus a couple of others changed regularly. Also Guinness, Heineken and Stella Artois. A comprehensive wine list has bottles from all corners of the globe.

This is a Wayside Inn serving food, all home-cooked on the premises, weekdays from 12 – 2.30 and 6 – 9, weekends from 12 noon. Typical starters roasted pepper and mushroom bruschetta, potted game pate and field mushrooms stuffed with bacon and cheese followed by moules mariniere et frites, Mediterranean vegetables and basil sauce and drunken duck served with an orange and Grand Marnier and a blackcurrant Cassis sauce. Also listed are various steaks, marinated shoulder of lamb, steak and ale pie, a hot chicken and bacon salad and smothered chicken – a butterfly breast topped with bacon, Cheddar cheese and a creamy mushroom, onion and brandy sauce. There is a separate childrens menu.

Dogs welcome in the garden and bar, children in family room and bar.

Open all day every day 11 – 11, (Sunday 10.30).

Special gourmet evenings are organised throughout the year.

Stuckton, nr. Fordingbridge. Tel: 01425 652489, Fax: 656144

Formerly a farmhouse built in 1863, The Three Lions was converted into a pub at the turn of the century. Since 1995 it has been personally run by the owners, Mike and Jayne Womersley, both experienced chefs, and is first and foremost an attractive restaurant renowned for its high standard and excellent food well plaudited in the press.

The bar is tiny mainly an area to enjoy a pre-dinner drink in front of the warm fire. The restaurant attractively furnished in lightwood has many cosy areas for intimate dining. There is a sunny garden at the front and side.

The well-stocked bar includes Lionheart from the Hampshire brewery plus Warsteiner Export and a 150-bin wine list.

The superb menu is listed daily on the blackboard and available Tuesday to Saturday 12 – 3 and 7 – 10, Sunday 12 – 2. Mike's philosophy is to create a more internationally flavoured menu based on the sound cooking techniques and expertise he has developed over the years using the finest quality locally grown ingredients. On any particular day you could expect to see sautéed lamb's kidneys and braised apricots, galette of smoked haddock, terrine of smoked chicken and gambas and seared scallops with an oriental dressing. Tempting main dishes include wild boar, apples and quince, sesame Quantock duck and mango, loin of roe buck and ceps, sautéed turbot, red wine and fennel, grilled sea bass and warm tomato, garlic vinaigrette and risotto of carnaroli rice, peas and parmesan. Sweets range from creme caramel, hot souffle and homemade sorbets to Jayne's chocolate pudding with vanilla sauce.

Well behaved children and dogs welcome.

Weekday opening times 12 – 3 and 7 – 10 Sunday 12 – 2. Closed Monday.

'The Lions' Den' offers three en-suite rooms.

Ringwood Road, Bransgore. Tel: 01425 672232. e-mail: info@3tuns.com

Situated close to the New Forest, the Three Tuns is a traditional 17th century pub with exposed beams, open fires and a friendly atmosphere. Outside there is an enclosed patio area with the beer garden to the rear being laid out informally and having the added attraction of a petanque terrain and views over open fields.

To complement the food, there is a good range of sensibly priced wines by the glass or bottle, keg beers, chilled lager and usually four well kept real ales like Ringwood Best and Fortyniner, Strongs Best and Youngs Special.

The pub has achieved the fine balance of maintaining the character and traditions of a good local as well as catering for the increasing market for exceptionally high quality, freshly prepared food which is both innovative and affordable. Cooked to order by highly qualified chefs the constantly changing selection is displayed daily on the blackboard. According to the season there could be moules mariniere with red Leicester and herbs and served with freshly baked bread followed by roast rack of English lamb with a red onion, orange and herb potato cake and a redcurrant and honey scented jus. Finally you could choose from the mouth watering dessert menu which would include items like deep fried ice cream with maple syrup. There is also a lighter snack menu available at lunchtimes, which is refreshingly different. On offer would be filo pastry basket filled with cherry tomatoes, pine nuts and buffalo mozzarella, with a lime and coriander oil or a soft Italian panini with smoked salmon, scrambled eggs, chives and black pepper. A full list of current menus and prices can be found on the web site.

Dogs welcome.

Opening times Monday to Saturday 11.30 – 2.30 and 6 – 11, Sunday 12 – 3 and 7 – 10.30. Booking advisable on Sunday.

Southampton Road, Lymington. Tel: 01590 672142

Originally known as the Crown Inn, the Tollhouse dates back at least to 1795 the name being derived from the turnpike tollgate cottage in the grounds which marked the northern entrance to Lymington and where tolls were collected mainly from salt traders leaving the town. In 1978 the name was changed to The Monkey House as the then landlord kept monkeys as pets which had a habit of pilfering from the customers. Whitbread chose the present name following refurbishment in the 1980's. The present tenants took over the inn a couple of years ago and promptly set about smartening everything up and a very good job they have done. The immaculate spacious main bar has a part polished wood floor, beamed ceiling, a piano in one corner and lots of brightly shining regalia. The second Tudor style bar, added in 1953, also has carpet and bare wooden floors and a large stone fireplace. A high beamed ceiling is decorated with the crowns of the Kings of England since 1066.

The well stocked bar includes three real ales presently Gales HSB, Ringwood Best and Wadworth 6X.

Bar snacks and an extensive home-cooked menu is available every day 12 – 2.30 and 6 – 9.30, the choice chalked daily on the blackboard. Expect to see 'Popeye' – sautéed mushrooms, garlic cream and spinach baked with goats cheese, peppered warm smoked mackerel set on leaves with creamed horseradish and caper sauce and home prepared deep fried Brie with cranberry sauce. Also Thai fish cakes set on noodles, rack of lamb, oven baked chicken supreme with red wine and mushroom sauce, fish pie, whole fresh local sea bass with lemon and parsley sauce, venison pie in red wine and a gammon steak, boiled with an orange glaze.

Dogs and families welcome.

Normal weekday opening times 12 – 3 and 5.30 – 11, all day Friday – Sunday. Three en-suite double rooms.

Hart Hill, Frost Lane, Hythe. Tel: 02380 842356.

The Travellers Rest can take a bit of finding but is well worth the search. From Hythe continue along Shore Road into Frost Lane, Hart Hill is on the left. This truly traditional white and black painted pub is located near the end of this narrow country road high above fields at the rear with views across the water. Footpaths including The Solent Way radiate just yards from the front. Steps at the front lead directly into the carpeted bar which has a small fireplace at one end and a brick fireplace at the other with a warm wood burning stove on a raised hearth. Furnishings consist of assorted tables, chairs and wooden settles. There are picnic benches on the lawn and a good children's play area.

The bar offers a complete range of drinks, which includes a choice of real ales from the Ringwood Brewery plus Wadworth 6X.

A small but adequate menu can be had 12 – 2 and 7 – 9.30 (not Monday evening) Sunday 12 – 2 only. Supplementing the sandwiches, jacket potatoes, and ploughman's are soup, egg mayonnaise, prawn cocktail, wings of fire, breaded mushrooms, prawn surfs and garlic bread. Main meals include sirloin steak, breaded scampi, gammon, breaded veal cutlets, boneless pork steaks and breaded lemon sole. There is a vegetable and pasta bake in a creamy sauce and pasta with tomato, mushroom and basil both served with garlic bread. Children have a choice between 'fishysarus', chicken 'teddies' and sausage and there are sweets to follow.

Dogs allowed in pub and garden. Children welcome.

Opening times Monday – Friday 11 – 2.30 Saturday 11 – 11, Sunday all day 12 – 10.30.

Minstead, nr. Cadnam. Tel: 02380 812137.

Minstead is referred to in the Doomsday Book as Mintestede (mint place). First records of the church are 1272. Originally thatched it is constructed from rubble-stone and bound with lime mortar. Inside there is an unusual three-decker pulpit, wooden galleries and private pews reserved for the wealthy, one even has its own fireplace. Conan Doyle, the creator of Sherlock Holmes is buried towards the rear of the graveyard.

Situated opposite the Green, the Trusty Servant is a typical village local with an interesting sign depicting a servant with a pig's head originating, it is believed, from Winchester College in the days when pupils had personal servants. The inn has undergone several refurbishments in the past few years and now has a small public bar at the front, lounge at the back heated by real fires and a very attractive candlelit restaurant and rear beer garden.

Four real ales presently offered by tenant Tony Walton include Ringwood Best, Wadworth 6X, Gales HSB and Fullers London Pride.

Good food is available 12 – 2 and 7 – 10, Saturday 12 – 2.30, Sunday all day 12 – 9. The comprehensive printed menu lists snacks and ten starters including the house speciality 'seafood chowder' accompanied by garlic bread. Fish dishes include steamed skate wing, whilst vegetarians have a choice of four meals. Pan roasted Barbary duck breast, grilled venison haunch, flash roast pheasant supreme, braised lamb shank and steaks are all on the menu together with home-made pies. Separate children's menu. New Forest ice cream is always available.

Children welcome, dogs in bar only.

Weekday opening times 11 – 11 (10.30 Sunday).

Four double and two single rooms all en-suite. English Tourist Board 3 crowns.

Burgate, Fordingbridge. Tel: 01425 652227. Fax 656207

The Tudor Rose is a delightful, half-timbered and thatched 14th century inn located just north of Fordingbridge. Although largely original with flagstones, heavy beams and a splendid 15th century open fireplace, the bar area has been opened up and warmly furnished with prints, paintings and countryside bric-a-brac. The minimum of doors exist to make things easier for the Cavalier ghost slain by the Roundheads, who regularly makes an appearance noisily slamming the door behind him. Picnic benches are neatly positioned in the very pretty front garden.

A well-kept range of real ales are always available with particular preference to the locals Ringwood Best and Ringwood Fortyniner.

This excellent eating house is operated under the entrepreneurial skills of Richard and Sonia Lowe. The imaginative menu contains an exciting range of starters like black pudding and bacon stack, engulfed with whole grain mustard and melted Cheddar, button mushrooms pan-fried in a cream and Stilton sauce served on a slice of toasted granary bread and warm breaded wedges of Brie served with a warm cranberry conserve. Main courses (almost 40) include all the traditional English fayre with an extensive range of dishes from around the world, all freshly prepared on the premises. They range from roasted tortelloni and turkey jalfraize to aromatic chicken tikka masala and vegetable moussaka. Customers travel from miles around to enjoy the 'Full Monty' – naked ribs of pork marinated with onion rings and fries, or the hot 'n' kicking Cajun chicken. The usual snacks of sandwiches, baguettes, ploughman's and jacket potatoes are also available.

Dogs and children equally welcome.

Monday to Friday opening times are 11 – 3 and 6 – 11, Saturday 11 –11 and Sunday 12 – 10 30.

Eling Hill, Totton. Tel: 02380 660837. Fax: 02380 865018.
e-mail: sylvabella&aol.com

The Village Bells is one of two pubs opposite each other at the junction of two lanes, both different but equally popular with the locals. Cosy rooms radiate left and right from the small, boarded passageway. Laid out for dining, both have low beamed ceilings, one has a small raised hearth, the other a warm wood burning stove. A separate carpeted room has tables and chairs, a high painted green ceiling and brick fireplace.

Although part of Merlin Inns, the pub is run as a freehouse offering a good range of real ales, four in winter six in summer which include Courage Best and two from the Ringwood brewery, Best Bitter and Old Thumper.

Food times are the same as opening with a serve your self lunchtime hotplate 12 - 2. Fish is the speciality. Apart from snacks like thick cut chunky sandwiches and homemade soups there is breaded whitebait, deep fried breaded Camembert and a house favourite – fresh crabmeat with prawns, topped with piped potato and a cheese sauce, served grilled in a scallop shell. Main course fish dishes listed are whole lobster, whole sea bass, moules mariniere and a seafood extravaganza – various crustaceans including king prawns, green lipped mussels and crab claws. Other dishes are chicken Mexican style, lasagne Romano, tuna and pasta bake plus various grills.

Children welcome, dogs in far left bar only.
Opening times 12 – 3 and 6 – 11, slightly earlier on Fridays. Normal Sunday hours.

Pike Hill, Lyndhurst. Tel: 02380 282113. Fax 01425 277454

Close to the police station, the Waterloo Arms can be found a short way along Pikes Hill off the Lyndhurst to Cadnam road. Dominated by a large stag's head on the front wall, this very attractive two-storey, white painted thatched pub dates from the 18th century, obvious upon entering when greeted by brick and dark wood panelled walls, a heavily beamed wooden ceiling and large inglenook fireplace with roaring winter log fire. Assorted furnishing include couches and comfortable armchairs in front of the fire. There is a large extended area at the rear, tastefully decorated with tables and chairs, beyond which is a patio and lawned beer garden. The pub is beautifully kept with good standards of service in a friendly, hospitable environment.

The bar stocks a full range of malt whiskies, cocktails, extensive wine list and a selection of real ales such as Ringwood Best, Fullers London Pride, Flowers Original and Green King Abbott.

The menu available 12 – 2.30 and 6 – 9.30 is popular with local businessmen especially lunchtimes. In addition to the set menu, imaginative daily specials might include soups like tomato and lentil or cream of broccoli and cauliflower, Sri Lanken chicken or beef and turkey stews, chilli, a choice of steaks, whole baked crab with garlic, wine and melted cheese, roast rump of lamb with redcurrant and a hearty Sunday roast.

Both children and dogs equally welcome.

Opening times 11.30 – 3 and 6 – 11.

Romsey Road, Cadnam. Tel: 02380 812277.

Renovated a few years ago the White Hart is a busy pub popular with locals and tourists alike. The comfortable atmospheric interior is split into three main areas. One has a red quarry stone floor covered by a large rug, part panelled walls and solid tables, benches and chairs in a light wood. A smaller bar has bare brick walls, a mix of old furniture and an attractive fireplace with wood burning stove. There are more tables near the bar and in a small pretty dining room overlooking the sunny front terrace. There is an attractive beer garden, play area for children and a skittle alley.

Personally run by the Emberley family, the highest pub traditions are maintained. Four real ales are usually available which include Morlands Old Speckled Hen, Wadworth 6X and Ringwood Best Bitter plus a constantly changing guest ale.

The White Hart is renowned for its food so much so that it was voted 'Hampshire Dining Pub of the year 2000'. Served all week 12 – 2 and 6 – 9.30 the main selection is listed daily on the blackboard. Typically there is a homemade soup, smoked salmon rosette, deep fried potato skins followed by supreme of chicken and vegetable rosti with tomato and herb sauce, noisettes of lamb with tagliatelle and roasted vegetables, garlic and rosemary sauce, chicken fajitas served with floured tortillas and 3 dips, steak and mushroom pudding with mushroom sauce, rib eye steak and chicken breast with light peppered sauce, Thai spiced duck, with timbale of rice and plum sauce, trio of sausages and mash with onion gravy, game casserole, braised rabbit and venison, medallions of pork on a mash with a tarragon cream, sweet and sour pork, whole Poole plaice, rolled lemon sole stuffed with crab and saffron with herb sauce and seafood lasagne. For those just wanting a snack there are ham and eggs, omelettes, homemade chilli, a vegetarian selection, open sandwiches and jacket potatoes.

Dogs on leads only, children if booked in with families.

Opening times 10 – 3 and 5.30 – 11, normal Sunday hours.

THE WHITE HORSE   83

Ringwood Road, Netley Marsh. Tel: 02380 862166.

Attractively painted in cream and green under a grey slate roof, this very popular village inn was once an old farmhouse. Character has been maintained in the beautifully kept interior, which has a slab floor at the front, a public area with dartboard and TV at one side and a carpeted dining area the other. Further comfortable dining areas at the side and back have an assortment of country style furnishings.

The inn is a Whitbread partnership offering a good choice of drinks and real ales such as Ringwood Best, London Pride, Flowers Original, Wadworth 6X and Gales HSB.

Good food can be selected from the blackboard available lunch times 12 – 2 and evenings 6 – 9, Sunday 7 – 9. The menu which includes additional meals in the evening lists dishes like deep fried whitebait, potato skins filled with cheese and bacon, spicy chicken wings, breaded mushrooms with garlic mayonnaise and traditional pate followed by breast of chicken in a chassuer sauce, grilled gammon steak, pork Jamaican stir fry. Also a chicken curry, grilled halibut steak with a Cumberland and mustard sauce, roast braised beef in Ringwood Bitter, lamb's liver, bacon and gravy and Shanghai style chicken stir fry with lemon and ginger. Various 'eat your way around the world' theme nights are held during the year. The Poacher's Pantry caters for spit roasts, BBQs etc.

Families and dogs welcome.

Open all day 11 – 11, usual Sunday hours.

THE WHITE ROSE HOTEL   84

Village Centre, Sway, nr. Lymington. Tel: 01590 682754. Fax: 682955

The White Rose is an imposing red-bricked family run Edwardian country house set in five acres in the centre of Sway offering a relaxed and friendly atmosphere. The bar, which overlooks the extensive rear lawns, is nicely decorated with cane furniture.

The well stocked bar includes two real ales Ringwood Best and True Glory.

The lunch time menu served between 12 – 2 is chalked daily on the blackboard and might include broccoli soup, sauté of chicken forester, garlic sausages with bubble and squeak, grilled fillet of haddock mornay, baked red snapper with seafood sauce and a poached fillet of salmon in red wine with capsicum and spring onion. Also steaks, ham and asparagus mornay plus traditional favourites like chilli, beef curry, homemade steak and kidney pie and homemade lasagne. There is a reasonably priced two-course lunch and a three-course Sunday lunch. For those just wanting a snack there are the usual sandwiches, ploughman's and jacket potatoes and a children's corner.

Opening times 11 – 2.30 and 6 – 11.

Twelve en-suite bedrooms with colour TV and tea making facilities.

Sopley, nr. Bransgore. Tel: 01425 672252

The very atmospheric thatched Woolpack dates from the middle of the 18th century and during the war was a popular meeting place for the aircrew stationed at the nearby RAF base at Sopley. It occupies an idyllic spot beside a tributary of the Avon where one can sit beside the stream or cross the bridge to the lawned garden. Inside there are several cosy rooms, heated by open fires which radiate from the central bar. An additional large conservatory provides extra space for family dining.

A Whitbread partnership, the bar has a good range of drinks and real ales like Flowers Original, Wadworth 6X and Ringwood Bitter.

An imaginative menu is available every day 11 – 2.30 and 7 – 9.30. Chalked on a series of boards there are starters of breaded Camembert with a warm red currant glaze and king prawns tossed in garlic cream also Dutch open rolls and ploughperson's. In addition to steak, Murphy's and mushroom pie, barbecue spare ribs and char-grilled steaks main meals include pork valentine with a herb and apple stuffing, chicken breast in a baby onion cream and Cognac sauce and braised steak Diana in brandy, mushroom tomato and cream sauce. Heading the sweet list is banoffi pie, toffee crunch, syrup sponge and spotted dick plus specials like homemade brulee topped with fresh strawberries and a homemade biscuit.

Children welcome, must remain seated at all times.

Pub open presently all day every day 11 – 11, Sunday 12 – 10.30.

Live music Wednesday.

Main Road, East Boldre, nr Beaulieu Tel: 01590 612331. Fax: 612003
e-mail: saxon@southampton-net.co.uk

Situated in the middle of the New Forest, the Turfcutters's Arms succeeds in being not only the village local, but also a destination pub for diners and parties. It is now a family-run pub with a warm friendly atmosphere. There is a large garden at the rear as shown in the photograph and ample parking both front and rear

The beer is some of the best kept in the Forest, usually including four real ales such as Ringwood Best and Flowers Original. Also available are mild, Guinness, Heineken, Stella, Boddingtons and Blackthorn Dry as well as Addlestones Cloudy cider plus many popular bottled beers and lagers.

A wide and varied menu of homemade food as well as an extensive specials board which usually includes dishes prepared with local game, is served every lunchtime between 12 and 2.30 evenings 6 – 9.30, Sunday 7 – 9. Most dishes are prepared on the premises and, where possible, cooked to order. Supplementing blackboard specials like sea bass pan fried in garlic butter and pesto pasta with sun dried tomatoes and salami, main course dishes include jacket potatoes, homemade pies, half shoulder of lamb, roast hock of pork, mixed grill, tuna and swordfish steaks. There are many vegetarian dishes as well as a children's menu.

Children are allowed in the pub if they are well behaved, as are dogs – the pub has a young Doberman named Zeberdee – don't worry, he is friendly if rather large.

The pub is open 11 – 3 and 6 – 11 weekdays, Sunday 12 – 3 and 7 – 10.30 but flexible on demand.

Double en-suite room available with a very comfy bed as well as a spare single bed. There is a small barn for parties and meetings for up to 40 people.

Avon, Nr. Christchurch. Tel: 01425 762646

Located four miles from Ringwood on the Christchurch road, this splendid country house standing in its own large grounds in part dates back to the eighteenth century and was once the home of Lord and Lady Manners. Furnished to a very high standard and heated by an open log fire in winter, the comfortable light wood panelled Tyrrells Bar which overlooks the gardens extends through to the dining room and to the outside terrace.

It is a freehouse presently offering Ringwood Best Bitter plus Murphy's, Heineken and Stella etc.

For simple snacks the bar menu lists jumbo sausages, chef's country house pate, ploughman's and sandwiches. More substantial meals are chalked daily on the blackboard and might include fisherman's pie, plaice fillets with mushrooms in a mornay sauce, fresh poached salmon with a dill sauce, seafood salad, Welsh rarebit on toasted French bread, grilled mushrooms, ham and asparagus mornay, lamb cutlet with a Cumberland sauce, French fries and petit pois, home-cooked cold gammon ham, chicken breast with a cream and curry sauce and stir fried vegetables in a sweet and sour sauce. Sweets include hazelnut meringue with a strawberry sauce, apple pie, sherry trifle. Sunday roast.

Families welcome, special room for children, no dogs.

Opening times Monday – Saturday 11 – 3 and 7 – 11, Sunday 12 – 3 and 7 10.30.

Undershore Road, Walhampton, Lymington. Tel: 01590 672517

Originally called the Waggon Ale House, the Waggon and Horses is a modernised, country-style pub with an open plan interior heated by an open fire. It is situated close to the Isle of Wight ferry on the Lymington River. The deeds of the building show that it dates back to 1643. In 1893 the pub witnessed a tragic shooting when local gamekeeper, Henry Card, proved unwittingly that it was possible to shoot oneself in the back. A plaque on the wall records that he left a widow and nine orphans. Outside there is a pretty patio with bench seats.

The pub is a Wadworth tenancy and the new licensees are continuing to maintain the very high standards. Presently on offer are the breweries 6X and IPA also Fosters, Kronenberg, a selection of country wines, malt whiskies and Stowford Press cider.

Dining times are from 12 – 2.30 weekdays, Saturday 12 – 2 and 6.30 – 9.30 (summer 12 – 9.30) and Sunday 12 – 2.30 and 7 – 9 (summer 12 – 9). Good all round pub grub is available together with the normal sandwiches etc. The constantly changing specials board might list a shoulder of lamb or half a roast chicken with sweet and sour sauce and various steaks plus fish which could include fresh crab, sea bass, sole and cod or plaice etc. A good range of bar snacks are available during the day and a full à la carte menu in the evenings Wednesday to Sunday.

Children are welcome in the pub, dogs in the garden.

Opening times 11 – 3 and 6 – 11, Friday, Saturday and Sunday all day in the summer 11 – 11.

Bisterne Close, Burley. Tel: 01425 402264. Fax: 01425 403588.

Away from the village centre, hidden behind the golf club, is the imposing White Buck Inn. A popular venue for horse riders and walkers, the pub is set in its own grounds where from the front bar, once three rooms you have a lovely outlook across the stately lawns. A slope leads gently to a comfortable plush dining room decorated in red and gold. Real log fires complete the ambience. There is a large car park.

The inn is owned by George Gale & Co, the Hampshire brewers, offering three of their ales – mid-brown HSB, the medium-bodied, deep golden brown GB and the light Butser Bitter, also a guest like Ringwood Bitter.

People come from all round the area to sample the very good food, which is all homemade on the premises from the freshest of ingredients. Available every day of the week 12 – 2 and 7 – 9 (Sunday 12 – 2.30), the menu, chalked daily on the blackboard, usually includes regular favourites like the White Buck curry dish of the day and homemade steak and kidney pudding plus daily specials such as breast of chicken in a clear peppercorn sauce served on a bed of spinach and roasted rainbow trout stuffed with lemon and coriander. Also listed plaice fillet with sun dried tomatoes and olive butter, Thai marinated sword fish steak, char-grilled and set on a bed of mangetout and traditional beef and Guinness pie. Salads are listed on a separate backboard as are the sweets, which range from homemade crumble of the day and treacle sponge to homemade bread and butter pudding and sticky toffee pudding. Sandwiches, etc. are available for those just wanting a snack.

Children and dogs equally welcome.

Opening times all day 11 – 11, Sunday 12 – 10.30.

En-suite accommodation with SKY TV.